Westerners Through Chinese Eyes

Edited by
Jianguang Wang

Foreign Languages Press

Beijing

First Edition 1990
Second Printing 1995
Third Printing 1998
Fourth Printing 2000

ISBN 7 – 119 – 01216 – 9

ⓒ1990 by Foreign Languages Press, Beijing, China

Published by Foreign Languages Press
24 Baiwanzhuang Road, Beijing 100037, China

Printed by Beijing Foreign Languages Printing House
19 Chegongzhuang Xilu, Beijing 100044, China

Distributed by China International Book Trading Corporation
35 Chegongzhuang Xilu, Beijing 100044, China
P. O. Box 399, Beijing, China

Printed in the People's Republic of China

Contents

Introduction

THE image of Westerners in Chinese eyes has undergone a gradual change. In modern times China was enslaved and humiliated by many Western countries. Atrocities committed by the Western invaders left incurable scars on the Chinese people of that time, and foreigners were called "overseas devils," a reflection of the deep hostility towards them. When the People's Republic of China was founded in 1949, it was not recognized by major Western powers. Furthermore, an economic blockade was enforced against China in the 1950s. In the absence of normal relations, the image of "overseas devils" lingered on for quite a long time. Descriptions of the havoc wrought on China by foreign invaders were found in school textbooks, movies, and news media. Teenagers were told how the "devils" used to bully the Chinese people and loot their motherland. It was not until the 1970s, when China opened itself to the outside world that the image of "overseas devils" gradually began to fade. A feature of the open policy was the outpouring of Chinese students and visiting scholars to Western developed countries, which made it possible for them to view Westerners and the Western world with their own eyes. This, together with the influx of Westerners to China, changed the old biased concept about Westerners. Students and scholars found that Westerners "are normal, not much different from us Chinese," and that all people, Westerners and Chinese, share "the common values of family, friendship, and love... despite their different cultural backgrounds and political systems,"   as written in "The Americans I Know."

Here in this unprecedented and original book, a kaleidoscopic Chinese view of Westerners is presented. Contributed by people from all walks of life, the twenty-seven essays and stories are divided geographically into two parts. Based on their personal experience, the writers, most of whom have been abroad or are now living, studying, or working abroad, describe Europeans in the first part, and North Americans in the second.

One believes that French women are the prettiest in Europe. Their concept of love is to pick it up and put it down easily. They never trouble themselves with useless worries. French men are experts in love. They know how to love and be loved and are able to make their beloved feel the happiness of love as well as the pride of love. But once their lovers fall in love with them and can no longer control themselves, French men resume their chauvinist ways.

Greeks are depicted as the vivacious people of a beautiful but poor land. They live easily — even at 12 midnight they are still lining up to buy *souvlaki*. They are careless about hygiene, dropping food, paper and waste everywhere. However, they have a deep affection for their nation and pride in their rich cultural and spiritual heritage.

"Scottish Fishermen" sings of the Scottish fishermen's sangfroid before disaster. The writer attributes this to the vast sea that has cleansed their minds of mean and vulgar thoughts, purified their hearts, leaving no room for fear, either of nature or man, to creep in.

"A Purse" describes a considerate, warm-hearted black American woman, whom the writer met only once for a short time, but whom she'll remember all her life.

In "She Loves Man, But Not Men", a pretty young Canadian woman claims to love China and the Chinese people, but when she cuts a small boy's left shin terribly with her skates, she doesn't even apologize but complains of the boy's getting into her way, adding that "Chinese people have a tendency of getting into other people's way."

Comparisons are made of Westerners and Chinese, with emphasis on the differences between them. In Finland, as the writer of "The Finnish Girl" says, children are influenced not by the family but by society. When they are young, they learn to face the society in which they will have to struggle to survive when they grow up. Therefore, they have a strong sense of competition, which Chinese children lack. Children brought up in the Chinese way, the writer says, are usually spoiled, weak-willed, slack in spirit and common in quality.

In "Miscellaneous Talks on the People of the East

and West", a large number of differences are listed. One example is personal service. In the West, the people who receive you are always polite and helpful. In China, although the slogan "Serve the People" can be seen everywhere, such behaviour is difficult to find. Almost all service workers put on a stern expression.

Comparisons are also made between Westerners. "The Melting Pot and the Mosaic: A Comparison of Americans and Canadians" provides many hints on how to tell an American from a Canadian, such as probing their attitudes towards multiculturalism and bilingualism. Canadians would be positive about these two concepts, whereas most Americans tend to favour a one-culture, one-language environment, the result of the melting-pot effect.

Some essays touch upon social problems in Western countries, such as in "Americans and Divorce". It is written by Chen Fan, who used to teach at Chengdu Teachers School and who left China for the United States in the spring of 1987 after she married Jim, an American archaeologist. In the eyes of many Chinese, Americans are fickle and few of them stick to their first marriage. Using her own marriage as an example, Chen Fan argues otherwise. She quotes Jim as saying that divorce is painful for Americans, but not dirty, and that it's better to be realistic and separate in a friendly way than to live together without love. She shows deep sympathy for those Chinese couples who want to divorce but cannot because of social pressures. She thinks that Americans, despite a high divorce rate, live a happier and more relaxed life than those loveless and hopeless Chinese couples.

In short, this book is a Chinese window through which readers can see Westerners of various types: affable, humorous, serious, motherly, fatherly, hypocritical, accommodating, thoughtful, greedy.... I sincerely hope that through these Chinese eyes, readers will better understand China and the Chinese people, Western countries and Western people.

Jianguang Wang
January 1990

I. Europe

The Beauty, the Water

Mei Yuan

MY Asian friends in Paris often ask me: "What is the difference between the Swiss and the French?" I reply somewhat facetiously: "French women are like water, so are the men; Swiss men are like mountains, so are the women."

Of course, this is only my personal feeling. But it seems to me that most French men lack the mettle of a mountain, and the majority of Swiss women are not feminine. I think, this phenomenon is connected with the geography of both countries. Switzerland is surrounded by mountains on all four sides and France has half of its territory by the sea. The national characteristics of the two countries are more or less affected by their natural surroundings.

When I was in Switzerland, I often thought Swiss men were the favourites of the Heaven. Besides the spirit of the mountain, they were also intelligent. Swiss men give you a sense of confidence; when they grasp your hand tightly, you know you can trust them completely. But, they are also sober-minded and arrogant. Passionless, they don't reach their hands out easily. As for Swiss women, they are the frankest as well as the least feminine in the

3

world. They are not hypocritical, never poke their noses into others' affairs, and do not have artificial manners. There is a lack of amazement and tenderness in their handsome appearance because all the charm of the bright mountains and delicate rivers has been grabbed by men. It was very hard for me to meet a charming woman in Switzerland.

I found the French women very pretty when I arrived in Paris. Women should be like water. French women are the prettiest in Europe, although some of them are built like men. A couple of times, I mistook a woman for a man, and vice versa. Some French men have long hair. Those with natural curves look like women because the style of their hair is not much different from that of women. When they wear shapeless overcoats, it is a real puzzle to distinguish their sex.

But another group of French women is very pretty, each woman with a charm of her own. The best of them are really as beautiful as water. But unfortunately, most of them lack a touch of nobility, or are too artificial. In World War II, European men suffered heavy casulties and there have been much more females than males among the babies born after the war. This made the men extremely conceited despite the fact that they received little of the charm between Heaven and Earth. In Paris, female clerks overwhelm their male colleagues in almost every office, not to mention department stores and factories, which are kingdoms of women.

There are too many divorced women and too many unmarried mothers in Paris. French men and women don't want to bind themselves with the yoke of marriage. Instead, they prefer to keep themselves free to enjoy love. French people care for their present enjoyment very much. The future is the future, why would they worry about it now? Because of the imbalance between boys and girls, only one in every three women has the chance to marry. Influenced by this environment, French women have seen things through; though they have become unmarried mothers, they still believe that those who have been loved are much happier than those who haven't. So they do not weep and trouble themselves with useless worries. Their concept of love is to pick it up and put it down easily.

French men are clever. They don't hide their love for a woman, and they always find the appropriate way to woo her. They know how to love and be loved and how to adjust the atmosphere. They are able to make their beloved feel the happiness of love as well as the pride of love. But once their lovers fall in love with them and can no longer control themselves, the men resume their chauvinist ways. I have a French friend who has all the charms admired by a woman. He likes me, but often makes me angry. To blunt his arrogance, I launched a war — a "cold war" — with him before we started our friendship. Every time we met, we saw each other as an enemy. But on other occasions, we behaved as if we were two naughty children. He was the person who made me feel angry, interested and happy, seeming to add two or three light notes into the music of my busy life. He is often circled by a group of women, making him the emperor of them all. The miracle is that these women can share his love peacefully. Very often, I see a beautiful woman on the arm of an ugly man, who also has an arrogant air. This reminds me of a vivid picture — a fresh flower sticking to a heap of dung. French men understand women very well. They know women's weaknesses — they need to be loved, no matter how beautiful they are and how superior they might be.

Romain Rolland gave a vivid description of the Paris gentlemen in his novel *Jean Christophe*. Rolland won the 1915 Nobel Prize, but he was not given much attention in his own country, probably because people don't like to have their negative characteristics revealed. But if the ugliness is not exposed and stopped, how can society improve?

Based on what I've seen and heard, I have no confidence in a French man's love. I found many French families are just like what Rolland described in his novel: the husband has a mistress while the wife has a lover. What is even more fantastic is that the husband and the lover, the wife and the mistress can get along harmoniously. They all agree not to be too serious and cause a divorce. Sometimes, I think the relationship between husband and wife resembles that between partners in a company. On the one hand, they co-operate with each other for their common interest, or even do something for the other side when necessary. On the other hand, they seek their own privacy and happiness. It seems unimaginable for me that even when a couple is deeply in love, they still have no desire to get married and remain devoted to each other to the end of their lives. Their philosophy is "to make yourself happy today." They often jest with me, saying that I always seek troubles for myself and don't know how to enjoy life.

When a couple of lovers decide to live together, few of them mean to get married. The female is not at all embarrassed when she announces the news; on the contrary, she is as excited as if she were going to be a bride. Their explanation is that only after living with someone can they find out if they are suited to each other. If not, they just leave, saving the complicated procedures of divorce. If both have the desire to remain together for the rest of their lives, it is never too late to get married.

This sounds reasonable. When a couple is in love, they may cover their own shortcomings so as to please the other. At the same time, they may accommodate themselves to the other's interests and habits. But once they get married and establish a closer relationship, their natures will be exposed. Gradually, there will be no more patience for accommodation. Very often, a married couple has to put up with each other to save face.

Last year, when I revisited Paris, I met an elegant French girl in my dorm. After talking for a while, we found we had many interests in common and instantly became good friends. One day, she told me excitedly that she was soon going to live with her boyfriend. Contrary to her expectations, my reaction was so cold that there was no sign I had just been told good news.

"Since you love each other so much, why don't you get married instead of just living together?" My question seemed unsuitable for her happy mood.

"We'll get married," she replied, still excited. "Remi said we live together first and get married two years later."

"Then, why don't you wait for two years to live together?"

"No. We can't wait any longer," she replied. "Remi says we've spent too much time on dating. But we both feel that we cannot be separated and we worry about each other a lot. So we must live together."

"But what if he will not marry you two years later when you already have a child?" I continued my disappointing pursuit.

"I think he will marry me because he loves me very much," she replied with a touch of emptiness on her face. "If he won't marry me, we have to end it. I'll find another man. I won't have any child before we get married formally."

I could not help saying, "Sometimes, the baby comes when you don't want it. The innocent child needs a father, anyway. And, are you sure the next man you love will agree to marry you if Remi doesn't and you separate from him? Marriage is the protection of a woman. An ordinary woman always hopes to have a happy family life."

"I'm trying to have a happy family life by living with Remi," she said, obviously not having gotten the real meaning of what I said.

Having no more to say, I gazed upon her quietly. Through her pretty face, I saw another visage — one of an unmarried mother I had known. She was nearly 21 years old, but already had two illegitimate children, one white, one black. I had wasted a lot of my sympathy for her because of the false, tragic story she made up. Of course, that was a vulgar and ignorant girl, but the woman right before my eyes had received a higher education.

In our later meetings, we tried to avoid topics such as marriage and living together, but I had the feeling that she had discussed the problem with Remi, who turned cold to me without any provocation. One night she came to see me, asking me to help her pack because she and Remi were going to London for a month's vacation before they started living together. Noticing my indifference, she began to ask for my opinion on every trifling thing, including which of her pajamas was more beautiful, which bathing suit, the yellow or the green she should take, which skirt the coat could match.... Seeing that she was as happy as a bride, I tried to help her choose.

The next day, Remi came to pick her up. When we hugged and said good-bye to each other, we both felt somewhat dejected. We were still good friends. But we all knew we might not see each other again. I understood that one can sacrifice a friend for love. As to Remi, he looked at me and I looked at him. We did not exchange a single word. I knew he thought I was interfering in their affairs, and I felt sorry for that, too. But I didn't want to ask him for pardon. By that time, I had obtained a better understanding of European men and women: they knew what they were doing and what could be the possible result. But they were willing to do it because they wanted to seize the pleasure of the moment. They would not entertain fears like the man in ancient China who worried all day and night that the sky might fall down.

The Lovely
Impoverished Land

Tham Yew Chin

G REECE, a country with agriculture as the main-
stay of its economy, is often branded by well-to-do
European nations as a poor nation. But the Greeks
I saw during my trip to Greece were not working
diligently to make a living.

They were living easily. None of those walking
in the street, either going to school or to work, was
in a hurry. They all walked slowly and talked
loudly.

In the Greek capital of Athens, coffee shops
dotted the streets everywhere with tables and chairs
lined up in the shadows of trees. When night came,
people crammed into the cafes. The trees swayed in
the breeze and the flowers spread their perfumed
aroma as patrons held heated discussions while
eating and drinking. What date was it that day?
Nobody cared!

A world soccer competition was under way at
that time. Every coffeehouse with a TV set was
crowded with·people, their eyes fixed to the screen
as if they knew nothing else. When a player scored

11

a goal, they shouted; when a goal was missed, they spat. The atmosphere was especially warm.

One night, after a day's sightseeing, I walked back to my hotel, tired. While crossing a street, I saw a long queue of people. Curiously, I went to see what was the matter. They were lining up to buy *souvlaki*, skewered barbecue pork! I looked at my watch; it was midnight!

Many Greeks are involved in small business. They set up stalls, selling all kinds of goods such as newspapers, periodicals, candies, postcards, milk, bread, eggs, and so on. There are as many as 3,000 shops of this kind in Athens alone. But the owners are not active in doing business. I saw many of them sitting there easily with their legs crossed, smoking, drinking coffee and watching TV. There are also many mobile stalls on streets and lanes, selling corn, sweet rolls, nuts and pickled olives. They never hawk their wares. Instead, they stand idly, as if they had nothing to do with the stalls they own.

The most interesting was the owner of a toy store who piled all his dolls at the door for sale. I picked up one and, as usual, began bargaining with him. "Please, Madame," he said with an exasperated expression, "I have put all my things on sale because I'm tired of hearing the tourists bargaining with me all day, always asking for 'discount, discount.' You want me to lower the price again? I tell you, I have leased my shop so that I can go back to my home in the country to raise pigs and do farming. I would die if I had to stay and deal with thousands of tourists like this."

Then he went into the shop without turning back, seeming to be afraid that he would suffocate if he stayed a minute longer.

Over the past few years, Greece's tourism industry has expanded and the number of tourists has increased remarkably. The Greeks are warm towards tourists. Though they may not offer their hands of friendship automatically, they give their help when they are asked.

If you ask someone the way, he or she will consider it a duty to tell you the details clearly and patiently.

One day, I wanted to go to a Chinese restaurant. I took out a map and asked a clerk at the hotel desk to tell me how to get there. He drew a line with a red pen to show the way and marked everything clearly. After we left the hotel, he again caught up with us to help call a taxi and explained to the driver in Greek.

I went to a colourful flower market on a rather warm day when there were not many tourists on the street. Some of the shop owners sang us lively Greek songs, others gave me a big yellow chrysanthemum or a sweet rose. With all this I forgot that I was visiting a flower market in a foreign country. Instead, I seemed to be walking in an old friend's garden.

One of the interesting things that stays in my memory was a Greek wedding I attended unexpectedly. One day at dusk I passed a church. Seeing many people bustling in, I entered it before I realized it was a wedding. The usher welcomed me with a warm smile, though, obviously, I was not one of the guests who had been invited. She gave me a coloured ribbon, a flower basket as small as a cup, and, to my amusement, she put a handful of rice in my palm.

With great jubilation, the bride and bridegroom came.

After the new couple expressed their willingness to marry, the people sang hymns. Then they threw rice at the newly married couple. Now I understood that rice grains meant good wishes, so I followed suit. As soon as I finished the rice in my hand, I was given another handful. White rice grains were flying in the church like falling snow flakes.

A little while later, the new couple found me and came up to me with big smiles. They greeted me in Greek. Not able to speak a single word of Greek, I just smiled back quietly and congratulated them by reaching out my hands. The bride kissed me on both cheeks. The warmth she exuded still seems to be there on my face today.

The sincere and straightforward characteristics of the Greeks are also shown in their expressions and loud voices. All of them, male and female, old and young, speak loudly and confidently.

The back side of my hotel in Athens faced a residential area. Every morning, the loud voices from over there served as the alarm to wake me up. You would think they were shouting and crying. In fact, they were just talking in their own houses. But their voices, like the sound of loud bells, penetrated the windows, and carried everywhere. In other places, such as restaurants, buses and elevators, they never talked in low voices. That was why it was so lively everywhere.

However, I was shocked to see that the Greeks are careless about hygiene.

I started my trip in Greece from Athens. From there, I went north to Alexandroupolis and south to the island of Crete. In big cities and small towns everywhere, I found that the Greeks didn't care much about public hygiene.

They dropped food, paper and waste everywhere. What made it even worse was that the Greeks were fond of fruit, especially olives. So there were fruit peels, shells and cores everywhere on the ground as if there had just been a carnival.

A small episode occurred which showed this lack of attention to cleanliness. One day I took a long-distance bus from Athens to Delphi, the religious centre of ancient Greece. I nibbled a lot of fruit and other food, putting the waste into a plastic bag. Then the old lady sitting beside me unexpectedly picked it up and threw it out the window without any hesitation. The garbage inside the bag spread everywhere into the air before falling to the ground. But she just sat there and smiled at me, seeming to be very proud of herself for her "good deed."

My memory of another small incident remains not only fresh but scary.

A man sitting in the bus was drinking his coffee. After he finished half of the cup, he poured the rest out the window, not even looking if anyone was there. The result was a spatter of hot "black rain." All I could do was to turn my head aside.

While not caring much about public hygiene, the Greeks have a very strong sense of patriotism. They are very proud of their rich cultural and spiritual heritage.

They talked about their sages and historical sites and openly expressed their pride in their nation.

A Greek waiter once told me that he went every weekend to the ancient theatre in Epidaurus, a 2 1/2 hour trip. The theatre was built in the 4th century B.C. Its seats, hewn out of rock, are arranged in a U shape. Their height increases gradually from the front to back rows. It remains a puzzle that though there is no acoustic equipment, the voice of a singer standing at the centre of the stage can be heard perfectly by an audience of several thousand.

The Greeks are proud of their brilliant past. How do they feel about their present situation?

Compared with other West European countries, Greece is poor and has many social problems.

While talking with the Greeks, I found they did not try to cover up these problems. But they did not criticize their country blindly. It was clear that their sharp criticism came out of their profound love for Greece.

A Greek lady once said: "We criticize it, but we'll never abandon it."

During my trip to Greece, I met many Greeks who had returned home from other countries. They had left originally because of economic difficulties. They made a living abroad, but didn't set down roots. When they got married, they looked for Greek spouses; they spoke Greek; they preferred Greek food. The strong sense of homeland makes Greece a powerful magnet for its sons and daughters overseas. Those who have achieved great success dream of returning home gloriously; those less successful ones also want to spend the rest of their lives in their hometowns.

I was deeply moved by their patriotism.

It is not easy to discover all of a foreign nation's special characteristics during a short trip. But I believe that the individual can reflect the society — through small matters you can see a person's major characteristics. Through the behaviour of many individuals, you can summarize the characteristics of a nation. So, every time I travel, I keep my eyes and ears wide open. What I've recorded and written can only represent my personal opinion.

I did my best to capture their reality when I observed, listened, and wrote about the Greek people.

The Mid-Summer Carnival

Tan Ni

As soon as I got down the train, I sensed the unusual atmosphere permeating the western Norwegian city of Bergen.

People were everywhere, all in strange clothes. Men and women, old and young, were dressed strangely and wore bright, colourful makeup. It seemed that characters from children's stories — fairies, heroes, demons and devils — had all walked out of their books and jumped into the street. Everything looked so unreal that it seemed I was touring a legendary world.

Downtown, the view was even grander and the atmosphere more enthusiastic. On the large square, grills had been built and the smell of barbecued food filled the air. Everyone, with either a bottle of beer or a popsicle in hand, swayed their hips and sang loudly. It seemed that a bomb of pleasure had just exploded in this city of 200,000 people, splashing happiness in the air and on the ground.

It was June 15. But what a festival was it?

"The Mid-Summer Carnival," a young man told me. "It was set as a festival of celebration last year."

Norway, in the northern hemisphere, has only

three months of warm weather each year. The other nine months are cold. What is even worse is that during the depths of winter the sun never comes out. Besides going to work or to school, people tend to stay at home the rest of the time. This colourless life makes the young feel depressed and the old lonely. So the Norwegians, old and young, all agreed that a touch of colour was needed in their lives. The Mid-Summer Carnival was thus established.

The mid-summer festival has enriched their lives. Although the celebration lasts for only one day, several months are spent on preparations, including discussions about the character each person is going to play and the special homemade costumes they will wear. During this process, people draw closer to each other and their social life expands. People are like snails, reaching out their feelers to probe the world outside their shells. Once there is such a goal to look forward to, everyone feels happier and more relaxed. The dark, bleak winter is no longer unendurable.

I had never seen any festival that could make the people of a whole city so enthusiastic as the Mid-Summer Carnival in Bergen. Infants, their tender faces painted into colourful cats by their parents, sat in their strollers. White-haired old ladies dressed as queens walked along the street with dignity escorted by their grandaughters. Charming girls, young wives, teenagers, grown men and families all did their best to create beautiful costumes.

Though it's widely welcomed, the Mid-Summer Carnival also brings problems, mainly caused by drunkards.

It gets dark very late in Bergen in summer, and it's still light at 10 p.m. Having seen enough of the carnival downtown, J and I decided to go to the quiet hills to get a view of the city.

The bus was packed. The almost drunk passengers were singing or joking in high spirits. We enjoyed the pleasant atmosphere and felt as happy as the rest of the people.

Because the bus was already full, the driver did not want to stop at the next bus stop. But before he realized it, two men dashed into the middle of the street. The driver slammed the brakes and the two crazy passengers jumped onto the bus immediately. One of them grabbed the driver by his collar and shouted at him: "You bastard. Why didn't you stop?" Sitting on the seat behind the driver, I smelled the alcohol on their breath. The driver did not struggle or argue, but the man continued shouting at him:

"Speak! You bastard, speak! Why didn't you stop the bus?"

At this moment, two other passengers came up and tried to stop them. Only after the two drunkards were pulled away from the driver could the bus start again.

All the passengers got off eventually. When the bus arrived in the mountain area, there were only J and I. The driver stopped the bus and turned around in his seat to speak to us.

"I'll stay here for half an hour," he told us kindly. "If you come back in time, you can take the same bus to go back down."

Then, he left his seat to pick up the empty bottles. Watching him bend down, I could not help saying:

"I feel very sorry for what happened just now."

"Oh, those stupid young men," he said with a deep sigh. "I hate this Mid-Summer Carnival. Nobody knows how many accidents were caused by drunkards last year. Bergen used to be a quiet city. But now it's all out of order."

He searched the seats and picked up more than a dozen empty bottles. Pointing at them, he knitted his brows and said:

"Look at this, how disgusting! Some people commit all kinds of violent crimes after drinking alcohol, including rape and robbery. You two had better not stay too long and go home early."

Following his advice, we spent only half an hour on the top of the hills and returned to town by the same bus.

It was almost midnight, but it was still clear and light. We waited at a bus stop downtown to transfer to another bus to the hotel.

Up came a man wearing a fur coat and a blue gauze skirt. The slit of the skirt was wide open, exposing his legs in nylon stockings. On his feet were women's soft leather shoes. His long face with a projecting jaw resembled Zhu Yuanzhang, the first emperor of the Ming Dynasty.

With a rolling gait, he walked up to a girl and unbuttoned his fur coat suddenly and showed his thin blouse. With an affectively sweet voice, he said:

"Look, is it beautiful?"

"Yes, it's very beautiful," the girl giggled and replied.

He was satisfied and touched the girl's cheek. Then, he turned to me. Smelling alcohol, I retreated a few steps. His face changed, his eyes shone fiercely. Pointing at the ground, he said to me: "Come back immediately! Come on and stand here!"

I returned obediently to where I had been standing.

He grasped J's beard and asked in a drunk voice, "What is this?"

"It's my beard. Haven't you seen one before?" J pretended to laugh lightly and pushed his hand away.

"Where did you come from?" He asked, pointing at my nose.

I stared at him with cold eyes and refused to answer his question. At the same time, I prayed that the bus would come as soon as possible.

He continued talking nonsense. Afraid that he would become violent, I did not dare to offend him and responded to him casually. The bus came at last. But at this moment, he grasped my hand mischievously and kissed it. His sticky saliva wet my hand. I flared up. Drawing back my hand desperately, I jumped onto the bus. He stood there and laughed wildly — a drunkard. After returning to the hotel, I washed my hand again and again. What an unpleasant experience!

The next morning, the city was as quiet as death. After the carnival, the central square was full of scraps of paper and bottles. Some of the bottles were smashed, leaving the broken bits glimmering in the sunshine. They seemed to be protesting silently against those who didn't restrain and respect themselves and had turned the jubilant festival foul.

A Chinese View of the English Mentality

Zhou Lisheng

A remote object may reveal surprising new features when observed at close range. So is the case of the English mentality, which has long been characterized as humorous, reserved and conservative. When this long-standing assumption is scrutinized in the light of the present-day reality of England, one finds that much of it is open to contention or in need of clarification.

People in China get to know the English mentality chiefly through novels, plays, dramas, movies, etc., and subsequently are inclined to entertain the notion that the British people they may contact one day must be, more or less, of this type. Some have even tried to crack a joke with their English guests after the usual preliminaries to ascertain the much-publicized English sense of humour but, to their surprise, only drew an indifferent response, the response of quite a different type of disposition from the one found in books. What is revealing about such anecdotes is the lack of affinity between the demeanour of these English guests and the typical English character people have been led to expect.

English author P.S. Tregidgo warns against generalization of his countrymen's character. He retorts with conviction that "A great deal of nonsense has been written about the character of a nation, chiefly because many observers, influenced by national pride and prejudices, feel irresistibly tempted to generalize about everything. In a nation of many millions of people, there are bound to be many different kinds: rich and poor, clever and stupid, good and bad, modest and conceited, patient and impatient, honest and dishonest. Moreover, a nation may develop a sort of collective character in its politics and literature which is not recognizable in individual people. Generalization therefore tends to be unrealistic and should be made, and accepted, with caution."

Apart from the improbability of discerning some highly hypothetical national character in individual people, there is also a great deal of misunderstanding as to the true meaning of the three widely accepted attributes of the English mentality. First, a good many people are apt to identify humour with laughter. Whatever is capable of inducing people to laugh is humour. And the ability to make or to appreciate a joke is regarded as a sense of humour. So they think. The fact is that the English sense of humour may not always be associated with laughter. The English sense of humour is an attitude to life rather than the mere ability to make people laugh or to laugh at jokes. Its central point is the capacity to jibe at one's own failures. It is the ability to face a formidable challenge good-humouredly, and, when one fails, to laugh at one's clumsiness in tackling it, at one's own faults and at one's awkward predicament. It has little to do with the common jokes which are often made at others' expense.

The notion of the English sense of humour has a long tradition, but it only became widespread after Charles Dickens' *Pickwick Papers* came out in the 1830s. This novel not only made the author famous, but also presented to the world, for the first time, a kind-hearted, lovable old English squire who was always doing good services for others while suffering one humiliation after another. Pickwick's enormous capacity for making the best of things, his magnanimous aptitude for laughing at his own failures won him great sympathy and produced the popular image of the English sense of humour. This image was further consolidated by the Irish playwright and critic Bernard Shaw through his satirical comedies, such as *Arms and the Man*, *Man and Superman*, and *Pygmalion*, all of which are full of paradoxical and humorous volubility. Perhaps it is not out of bounds to infer that the notion of the English sense of humour is a literary creation rather than a true reflection of national character. In present-day England, no one can possibly find a prototype of Pickwick, nor could you have done so even in Dickens' days. Experience has shown that to approach real human beings, who are so diverse in all respects, with some fixed literary image is both unrealistic and misleadingly fanciful.

While the English sense of humour is highly praised at home and partially misunderstood abroad, the other quality of the English mentality, reserve, is widely criticized and condemned as being uncommunicative and unsympathetic towards others. Such an accusation is not fair at all. If one examines what this English reserve is all about, one may not be so critical. To English people, loud talk in public places is distasteful. Blunt questions about others' age, income, private life or where or when or how one buys his or her clothes at what cost, etc., are all considered ill-bred. People may work together for years without knowing each other's hobbies. In short, each is for himself or herself with no concern about others' fortune or misfortune. This self-centred mentality, or egoism, is the product of capitalism, and is manifest in all developed capitalist countries, not just in Britain. There is no ground to condemn the English for a public norm of conduct so widely accepted throughout the capitalist world.

On the other hand, the word "reserve" implies self-control in speech and behaviour, reluctance to show one's feelings and unwillingness to take part in public events. All this gives one the impression that the English must be rather dull. Nothing could be further from the truth. In fact, they are fond of all sorts of public events. People of all ages pursue different kinds of amusement. The Lord Mayor's Parade each year through the busy centre of London, the parade of obsolete cars dating back to the turn of the century, horse races, dog races, sports competitions, beauty contests, walking tours, all these activities show no vestige of the much-criticized English reserve. Indeed, it is no exaggeration to say that the roaring, the yelling, the hysteria demonstrated in English football stadiums can hardly be rivalled by any people in the East.

Of the three commonly alleged attributes of English mentality, conservatism has probably given rise to a wider range of interpretations. It is common for the people in the developing countries to look at it as a sin, the sin of refusing to move along with the times. To them, conservatism is the exact equivalent of obstinacy. From a moderate point of view, people in the West regard the English as being conservative mainly on the assumption that social changes have been conspicuously slow in England. One is not only amazed to watch the virtually medieval royal procession but also bewildered to see Members of Parliament debating in the same venerable houses their predecessors did over four hundred years ago, with the Speaker wearing the same old wig over his shoulders even in the heat of summer, and the MPs fidgeting on the same old long, unpainted benches facing each other without any arm-rests at all. Couldn't some innovations be made to bring things up to date? One is bound to raise objections to these English eccentricities. Yet, the English or, to be exact, the influential circle, think otherwise. These people have a strong sense of nostalgia for what has been extolled as the glorious tradition of England. The phrase "the good old days" rings frequently in one's ears. To conserve what is good or familiar in their lifestyle, so they argue, is something rational, something to be proud of. So much so that a British political party is proud to call itself "the Conservative Party."

However, if we look through this kaleidoscope of royalist trappings and political antiquities, we shall see that they are preserved to remind the world that England was the first to introduce parliamentarism out of monarchism, and that England is able to sustain an intricate coexistence between the two. In modern times, conservatism in politics is esteemed mostly by the upper class with vested interests. The broad masses, especially the younger generation, have little enthusiasm for it and are fully aware of the fact that all this studied ostentation is supported at the cost of the taxpayers. One hears constant grumbles about royal extravagances, some mild, some hostile, and mostly ironical. Therefore, it is apparent that conservatism is a rarity of the few rather than an inclusive label for all.

Admittedly, the English have been slow to adopt rational reforms such as the metric system, decimal money and the twenty-four hour clock in communications. But this is a general tendency in most countries of the world. The English are not particularly slow in this respect. There are a large number of century-old customs still adhered to or even reinforced in many countries such as the black veils worn by women in the Arab world, the burning alive of widows with their dead husbands in some Indian states and many other horrifying practices.

In the last few decades, with the disintegration of the British Empire, the English mentality has undergone many observable changes. For the haughty dignitaries high up the social ladder, the foundation that fosters their conservatism and superiority complex is visibly dwindling. Instead of being comfortably seated at home to receive foreign envoys to talk things over in London, they now have to travel far to present Britain's case without the privileges of reciprocity. The ordinary people's outlook is shifting from what it used to be. The traditionally popular image of a slim, agile gentleman wearing a bowler hat and carrying an umbrella on his arm is no longer a model, but a funny-looking caricature. Clothing styles are moving away from formality towards informality. Rubber shoes, sportswear and even overalls are now thought fit for a gentleman's outdoor wear. Such a change of taste was unthinkable a couple of decades ago, and is challenging the predominance of dark grey business suits, hitherto the prevailing clothing for men. English women are now more receptive to foreign food, particularly Chinese, which is becoming a welcome addition to the English diet. Interestingly enough, as over one million foreign tourists pour into England during the holiday season every year, many English homes in seaside resorts and other scenic spots are open, seven days a week, to receive paying guests. However much reserve there once might have been in these English homes, money making has certainly helped get rid of it.

A foreigner from the East will find on his arrival in England that his preconceived image of John Bull is out of date. What he has learned about the English mentality from his instruction manual is likely to be unsuited to the people he meets. By and large, the people he does business with are earnest, courteous, and accommodating.

In conclusion, it may be said that a nation's mentality is such a diverse and changing phenomenon that it can only be treated on a case-by-case basis with each one's specific social status taken into consideration. To regard a nation's mentality as a fixed monolith is to run counter to the truth that variety is the law of nature.

Scottish Fishermen

Diana Shen

THE ringing of the telephone broke into our conversation. Maggie's aunt picked up the phone. Instantly, her face changed colour, "What? All of the crew?! ..." Her hand fell down, and without raising her eyes, she said in a low voice, "Our ship has run up on rocks; all the crew are dead." I cried out in shock.

This was in the winter of 1984 in a fishing village on the northern coast of Scotland, where Maggie — a friend whom I had met at the University of Edinburgh — was born and brought up. She had asked me to come with her for a short holiday. The third day after our arrival we were invited to high tea by her aunt, from whom we first found out about the tragedy.

Fishermen from Scottish villages are often related in one way or another. The shipwrecked crew were all distant relatives of Maggie. There was a tense atmosphere in the room. "That's really a tragedy!" Maggie said, "Maybe she'll never be able to get married again." Maggie was addressing her aunt. "Oh, yes," the aunt assented, looking the very picture of gloominess. Turning towards me, Maggie began to explain that they were talking about the wife of one of the dead fishermen. She was a young woman, just turned 23, whose former husband had been killed a year before, leaving behind this widow and two children. Six months later she was remarried and now pregnant. Who would have thought her new husband would be buried in the same stretch of water! Who would dare to take into his arms such an ill-starred woman, even if she still wanted to marry again? "But she has to marry somebody. Otherwise, how could she possibly survive?" her aunt cut in.

I was immersed in this tragedy. Suddenly a sense of fate's injustice seized me. They have met with disaster, while I am sitting snugly and comfortably by the fireside. I must seek adventure in defiance of the sea! With this impulse swelling my heart, I put forward a request to join a fishing trip. Scottish people are noted for their warm-hearted hospitality; they seldom turn down a request from their guests. Though my demand sounded unreasonable, when they saw I was in earnest, they agreed to arrange such a trip for me (of course with my safety guaranteed).

Soon after we returned to Maggie's home, there was a ring from Maggie's aunt, telling us that we could board a boat that was sailing to another port the next morning for maintenance. Maggie's mother at once sought out thick jeans for me to guard against the sea wind, muttering all the time advice to me about safety measures. This typical Scottish fisherwoman was very industrious and stoic. Her sincerity and simplicity left a deep impression on me. At our first meeting, she had only nodded at me and came over to help carry my luggage without uttering a word of welcome, thus making me feel she was a bit standoffish. It was only when we became more familiar with each other that I got to know her better. More and more I was touched by her deep affection and concern for me. Indeed, she had not a bit of formal graciousness but was very warm.

All through the night I was tense and excited. Quite unexpectedly, the next morning the sea was calm. Maggie and I got on a mini-bus which picked up the crewmen from door to door, to take them to the fishing-boat. Husbands got on the bus, with wives and children at the gate waving good-bye and silently watching the bus carrying them farther and farther away. The disaster that hit yesterday still weighed heavily on me. Those farewell scenes could not but steep my heart in gloom and sadness. Yet on the bus the ship's crew were talking and laughing all the way as if there had been no accident. Why such lightheartedness? I was quite bewildered. I knew those men were related to the crew who had been swallowed by the sea the day before — why didn't they show the least sign of sorrow and mourning? I whispered this question to Maggie, who answered that they were accustomed to it. Every month, every year, ships sink, men perish, but one has to live on. There's no use crying over the mishap. Such largeness of mind was another lesson these sailors taught me.

We boarded a medium-sized motorized sailing boat. The crew were very enthusiastic and hospitable to their foreign guest. A big, bearded crewman, patting me on the shoulder, said: "You are indeed a lucky girl. You are enjoying a special privilege. Do you know that in the past, cats, rats, and women were not allowed on board, because they brought bad luck with them?" I couldn't refrain from laughing aloud. Who could have supposed that Scottish fishermen would be so superstitious? In their struggle against nature, men were so weak in wisdom and strength that they had to attribute ungovernable natural calamities to animals and women.

I went down to the cabin with several crewmen. One of them took out a bottle of whisky, from which we sipped mouthfuls in turn. A while later, another crewman came in with a dish of broiled fish in hand. He was having breakfast. The crewman standing beside me stepped over to him, took his fork and helped himself to a big slice. Then another came over and also ate a mouthful. In this way, with the same fork, we "carved off" the same fish. We drank and talked in an amicable atmosphere. I found the Scottish fishermen were not inclined to lavish me with loads of food. They asked if I wanted a helping of something. If I said no, they wouldn't press me to take it. When I had meals at Maggie's, her mother always gave me large helpings of the best food. But after I had finished my share, she wouldn't automatically give me more; if I wanted more, I must help myself to it. Not having to behave ceremoniously, I felt more free and at home.

Returning to the deck, I viewed the fascinating scenery. The boundless sky and the gently rippling sea melted into one softness. In this blue, tranquil embrace, our boat was slowly and quietly moving on. Yet the shipwreck with all souls lost happened just yesterday! Who could say for certain that this blissful scene in which we found ourselves would not be fostering in its womb a sudden bursting storm? My vision gradually dimmed. Before my eyes were vast, ferocious waves, and threatening reeds and rocks; the fishing boat struggling in despair now on the crest of the waves, now in the deep vale.... A fit of cackling laughter suddenly interrupted my reverie. Looking back over my shoulder, I found Maggie and several crewmen were commenting on something with much gesturing. I asked Maggie what was the matter. She said: "These jeans fit you to a T. They were admiring your hips." I didn't mind it so much. Really, such vulgar jokes had been in my ears for some time. Two days before, Maggie's parents had been discussing the preparations for the wedding of Maggie's cousin with some relatives. They wanted to invite me to the wedding ceremony, but since Maggie's husband would also come, they had to find another place for me to stay. Maggie's aunt cordially invited me to stay at her home. Quite unexpectedly, like a bolt from the blue, Maggie's uncle blurted out: "If you come to us, you'll have to sleep with me." I was taken aback. How could he crack such a low joke?

I cast a look at Maggie's aunt and the others who were present. Nobody seemed to have noticed the remark. Only the uncle himself must have sensed he had gone too far, and he looked terribly embarrassed — after all I was a Chinese, a foreign guest. After that he never once looked at me. In order to ease his embarrassments, I bade him an especially warm farewell. Still he didn't raise his eyes to look at me. I felt quite ill at ease for his sake. Just as in the rural and fishing villages in China, a dull, monotonous life drives people to seek pleasure from crude jokes, but there is not the least bit of ill intention from the man who makes them. From the embarrassment of Maggie's uncle I came to understand the Scottish fishermen's good and simple nature. He thought his joke had hurt me, and was mortified over it.

I chatted with some crewmen. They were full of curiosity, especially about China. They fired questions at me one after another. I found them very talkative, their topics covering everything. Those who had voyaged over the oceans to far distant ports were especially proud of their experiences and would talk copiously about the people and customs of those foreign countries. I could not shake the disaster of the day before from my mind, but they seemed unaffected by it. These sturdy-armed, stout-waisted seamen loved the sea, they loved life. Perhaps the vast sea had cleaned their minds of mean and vulgar thoughts, purified their hearts and left no room for fear, caused either by nature or man, to creep in.

The smooth sailing ended. We landed at another port, where the air was thick with the stench of fish.

Everywhere there were heaps of fish and lobsters waiting to be processed and shipped. In Scotland, surrounded on three sides by the sea, fishing is a very important industry. Shops selling fish and chips were to be found at every turn. Maggie and I entered one, and ordered lunch. On the counter lay that day's "Scotsman." We both noticed on its front page the news of the preceding day's shipwreck with an eye-catching splash headline. Though the fish was very fresh, I had no appetite. The fish was caught at the cost of Scottish fishermen's lives! Maggie was eating calmly.

After lunch, we returned to the fishing village, which was peaceful and restful. Everything went on as before. It seemed Scottish fishermen had a remarkable power to bear up after tragic shipwrecks. Once the shock was over, they calmed down and went about their business as usual. "We have to live with it," everybody said.

During my stay in the small fishing village, I found some striking resemblances between it and our Chinese countryside. This village, bound together by blood ties, set great store by tradition. In its small post office I saw some postcards, most of them black-and-white photos of this village as it was 100 years ago. At that time it was dilapidated, a sharp contrast to the many new buildings of today. But how could one forget the homes of one's ancestors? These photos were kept as treasures and printed into postcards for posterity for the villagers to remember their forefathers. Older people in the village were held in great respect. Young men and women were more conservative in terms of sex than city folks. Maggie, who had grown up in this village, had been deeply influenced by convention. At sixteen she fell in love with a boy but refused to have sexual relations with him; it was her belief that a girl should still have her virginity before wedlock. Later, she got married in Edinburgh. In this big city, pressured from every side by modern ideas, her conservatism gradually gave way and, thinking back to her early first love, she felt somewhat regretful that her old-fashioned values had deprived her of her rightful pleasure. Maggie represented the younger generation aspiring after a new life. Though the older generation was content with its lot, there was no lack of young men and women— dissatisfied with the vapidness and stuffiness of village life — who left to seek a new way. Some went to nearby towns to work part-time, some went to big cities to hunt for a job. Maggie was then in her third year in the History Department of Edinburgh University. Many years of city life and higher education had greatly broadened her vision and her outlook. She felt her native fishing village too small and narrow, too full of "local" tang. However, at the same time, she had a deep-rooted love for her hometown. For her dissertation, she chose the development of her village as the topic. As one of the few villagers to go to university, Maggie was made much of and looked up to. Her parents and relatives prided themselves on this young woman, and she herself was also filled with the feeling of "returning home in glory and splendour."

The villagers were all ingenuous, kind-hearted people. When one got into trouble, all the others would come to his aid. But they liked to poke their noses into others' affairs, too. This had something to do with the poverty of their spiritual life. Though every two or three days people might drive 10 kilometres to a town to do shopping and seek some recreation, the life was rather dull. Thus gossiping and commenting on one's neighbours' words and deeds became a pastime.

The vacation came to an end. Maggie and I said good-bye to the fishing village and went back to our university. The shadow cast over my heart by the shipwreck gradually thinned away, but the Scottish fishermen's sangfroid in the face of disaster was deeply engraved on my mind. These courageous, liberal-minded, confident fishermen, who earned their bread and supported their families by the sweat of their brows, lived valiantly with a free, defiant spirit. I loved those people of the Scottish fishing village. They were so simple and sincere, so frank and enthusiastic towards others. Their friendship will live forever in my heart.

Queen of the Secretaries

Yu Xiang

Ms. Magi, the secretary of the International School of Trieste in Italy, is a very bright and capable woman, who is always full of energy and vigour. Warmness towards others and a never fading smile were the first images I had of her and they have never changed. I came to the school in January 1986 as its first Chinese student and everything was unfamiliar to me at the beginning. Furthermore, I did not speak any English at that time. So I often bothered Ms. Magi with various matters. She always listened to me with patience, watched me gesturing, and then kept guessing until she finally understood what I wanted to say.

The school was quite far from the city centre, so there was a school bus running every day. Ms. Magi was in charge of supervising the students on the bus. Whenever she appeared in front of the school bus, parents circled her and bombarded her with dozens of questions. Ms. Magi always listened attentively and gave short, clear-cut answers in fluent English or Italian. Only two or three minutes were usually needed before all parents left with satisfaction. In order to look after the students she never sat down on the bus — and that probably helped her to keep her beautiful figure in even better shape. Even though she read the newspaper most of the time, she never missed any of the children who were supposed to take the bus to school. Every afternoon, when the bus came back to the city centre, she waited until all parents picked up their children. Only then did she leave, feeling at ease. When I first came, I was not used to riding the bus for long distances, especially uphill. So Ms. Magi put me in the front row until I finally got used to it.

Ms. Magi's daily work load was very heavy, evident from her hasty footsteps. She used the telephone, typewriter and photocopy machine all day long. Using the telephone, she communicated with parents and many other institutions. We often saw her with the phone on her shoulder and writing swiftly at the same time. The photocopy machine in her office was used by Ms. Magi and many other teachers and students. Because many people used it every day, it often broke down. To make sure that all students took good care of it, she put this note on the photocopier:

> "This machine is a very good baby, but like many other babies, it needs tender care...
>
> mom"

That just shows how she was able to derive fun from her heavy and endless work load.

Ms. Magi did not teach but once, when the bell rang and all other teachers had taken their students to the classroom, Mr. Anaice, our science teacher, still had not shown up. Ms. Magi came to the classroom to review the lesson we had studied the day before.

She was not a tutor, either, but in the eyes of the students, she was our general tutor. No matter which grade, whenever students had any problems, they went to Ms. Magi, as if only she could solve them. One day, when Franz-Oliver was having his birthday party, he forgot to buy candies and went to Ms. Magi for help. She told him not to worry, and at noon when he came to the cafeteria she had already prepared the candy. Even when small children wet their trousers, they went to Ms. Magi. When we did not feel very well, or hurt ourselves, we asked her for help, too. She was in charge of everything, as if she were our mother.

One day in March, when we were all studying in the classrooms, the alarm suddenly rang. Before we understood what had happened, Ms. Magi rushed into the room and told us to leave the school building immediately. From her anxious look, we knew something extraordinary must have happened. In a short time, we were all gathered in the nearby gymnasium. Some people said it was a fire drill, others said the school was really on fire. What had actually happened, no one knew. Two hours passed, we began to feel hungry. Just then, our director, Mr. Metzger, came. He told us that someone had phoned the school, saying there was a bomb in the computer room that would explode in two minutes. That was why we had moved to the gym. Ms. Magi and the bomb detectors then searched through the school while we waited. Another half hour passed before Ms. Magi appeared in front of us, full of energy and vigour. From her smile, we knew everything was OK.

Afterwards, we learned that when Ms. Magi had received the phone call she was really astonished. With her years of experience, she had thought that it might be a bad joke but the lives of the teachers and the students had to be taken into consideration. So she rang the alarm and told all classes to leave the school building. When everyone was transferred safely to the gym, she and Mr. Metzger stayed in the school, checking carefully if there were still students left inside. Then she called the police, the fire brigade, and the bomb squad. She did not leave her post for a minute. Everyone admired her composure and disregard for danger. We all praised her as the hero of the school.

In May 1987, when it was Ms. Magi's birthday, the teachers gave her a gift of a jean shirt and a big birthday card with "Queen of the Secretaries" written on it. She was very pleased and said that she would hang it in her bedroom and look at it every day. I think "Queen of the Secretaries" was a very good appraisal for her years of hard work.

A Professor I Met in Germany

Feng Yuzhu

W HEN I first arrived in the Federal Republic of Germany, some girls living in the same dormitory building recommended that I take a course with a certain German literature professor. They said he was a serious person, had a wide range of knowledge and taught very well. Since I wanted to have precisely this kind of professor I decided to take his course. Knowing he gave counselling every Thursday, I went to see him.

I walked into his office quietly. The door closed slowly behind me. With that click, I couldn't help getting a little nervous. It was the first time I had talked with the professor. How could I express my thoughts clearly and let him agree to me taking his course? I felt my heart beating faster and faster as I approached him. I finally plucked up my courage and sat down in front of him.

Hearing my introduction, he lifted his eyes from a large pile of books on the table and looked at me with a casual smile. He first praised my German and then asked my plans. I had meant to tell him that I only planned to sit in on some of his classes to improve myself. But after he recommended a detailed list of books I readily promised to attend his classes and take his tests.

I still feel puzzled why I suddenly changed my original intention. Was it because his mild tone made it easy to trust him or that his plain clothing made an impression on me? Who knows?

When he went out to look for some books in a library next door, I had time to examine his office. I have been to many German professors' offices that are beautifully decorated. Most professors have their own private secretaries and their offices are full of colourful flowers. But this office was almost empty except for a table, a typewriter and a clothes stand. Only the books and teaching materials piled high on the table and the big leather briefcase at the corner of the table reminded me that he was a professor.

At the beginning, I was not accustomed to his way of teaching. I am a teacher too. At home I always stand in front of the blackboard, talk endlessly and write a lot. After two hours, I'm usually tired. My clothes and my hands are white with the chalk powder. But this professor was different. He sat in a chair and lay back comfortably with his eyes closed and a pipe in his mouth. Whenever I looked at him in this way, I often wanted to laugh. I really couldn't understand what was so unique about his class and different about his teaching. But after several classes, I came to realize they were very interesting and that he taught wonderfully indeed.

Strange to say, he never wrote on the blackboard nor pointed out what a certain book said about a writer. He seldom gave us a list of books to read. Instead, he often talked on and on slowly and softly like an old man telling stories to the kids. In a two-hour class he could expand your imagination and make you understand the ideological views of writers and critics. Sometimes he quoted books but never read from them. He recited those quotations as if he had the book right in class. Everyone admired his amazing memory and supreme literary technique. I also discovered that whenever he recited, he became so excited that his hands shook slightly, his eyes sparkled and his cheeks flushed. At this moment he would always take out his favourite pipe and light it slowly. I guessed he was not really enjoying the smoke of the burning tobacco but was intoxicated with self-satisfaction. Perhaps his emotion had an effect on me, who normally hates smoke. I felt he was different from others. Even the smoke he puffed out thickened the air with a special sweet smell.

I was the only foreign student in the class, so he gave special consideration to me. When the time came for us to write papers, he allowed me to choose the subject and lent me reference books that only teachers could borrow. When I started writing my papers I had to go to see him frequently about some points. Every time I went, he treated me warmly and pointed out where some of my views were incorrect or not comprehensive enough and suggested what books to read to improve my knowledge. Sometimes on Sundays he called me on the phone to tell me about a new viewpoint he had come across. Other times after class he handed me a note on which a sentence from some scholar or researcher was written. To express my gratitude for his help, I presented him with a very nice terracotta replica I brought from Xi'an. He held it in his hands cautiously, looked it up and down closely for quite a while and finally nodded his head and said: "Thank you, thank you very much." I could tell from his eyes that he liked it.

With the deepening of our relationship we talked more and more. Every time we met to discuss my paper we spent some time chit-chatting. He asked me about my study, work and life in China and I described the enthusiasm of Chinese scholars for German literature. However, he seldom asked about my family and never mentioned a word about his private life. At that time I thought he refrained from talking about himself in the re- strained manner most German people have. I re- membered that when I was a college student at home my teacher once warned us never to talk to Germans about personal concerns such as age and marriage, for it would be socially awkward. So I followed my teacher's instructions and I was very careful to keep away from sensitive questions.

My professor impressed me as a plain and seri- ous person. Whenever I came to his class, I noticed that he always wore the same dark gray clothes and carried the big leather briefcase. The quality of his clothes was not good but nobody in our class cared.

On the contrary, we thought it was his habit and besides, there were no regulations that professors must come to class in decent clothes or suits. I also noticed that even the chairman of the Literature Department did not like formal clothes, but wore jeans like most of the young people and rode his bicycle to school. It was a surprise to see other lecturers in the department in suits. Perhaps they thought they would gain more respect from the students that way.

Later I discovered that my professor did not have his own car but came and went by riding with one of his students. I felt this was a little strange. In this country of cars, there were few professors who did not drive.

One day at the end of June I went to the classroom on the fourth floor. As soon as I entered the room, I felt something unusual. My professor didn't wear his dark gray clothes but was dressed in black. His tightly closed lips set off by the snow-white shirt made him look more serious, firm and persistent. I looked at the other students curiously to see what had happened. But they sat quietly in their own seats and no one said a single word. The usual bustling atmosphere before a class was absent.

I dared not ask any questions, but slowly walked to my seat and put my books down. What on earth was happening here? I turned to Miss Korla beside me with a puzzled look. It seemed that she had no interest in answering my questions, but sat still and kept murmuring "Schade, wirklich schade!" (What a pity!) to herself again and again. I watched her and listened but I still didn't understand what she meant.

When the class began, all of us were soon carried away by the professor's lesson. I quickly drove those question marks out of my mind and concentrated on his teaching. That day everyone got a pile of materials introducing major writers and critics in the history of literature and a bibliography of reference books. I was surprised because in the whole semester he hadn't given us any material except for some very important quotations. "What's the matter today? Why did he suddenly give us so much material and who helped him?" I was pondering this so hard that I didn't hear what he talked about in class. I was alarmed and nervous and had an ominous feeling about the future.

The class ended an hour later than usual. Before he left he pointed at a notice pasted on the door and said he hoped we would be on time. Then he turned and stepped out of the room.

Immediately we rushed forward and gathered around the door. I pushed to the front and saw the notice for a farewell party for the professor. Not until then did I suddenly realize why he had come in new clothes and why he gave us so much material. Beside the notice there was a piece of paper on which we could write down what kind of food we would bring to the party. I quickly took out my pen and wrote my name under the column of cold dishes. Nobody left for the moment. The small, and narrow corridor was filled with students. Some sat on the floor, some stood carrying on endless discussions. I was terribly upset so I didn't pay much attention to what they said. I only overheard that my professor had to leave because another professor who had been invited to teach in a foreign country for three years would be coming back in a few days. I was not clear on why when one professor came back the other had to leave. I rode my bicycle directly to the nearest supermarket and bought what I needed for making salad.

That evening I tried to read a book, but after many pages I didn't know what I had read. I gave up and decided to wash some clothes. I couldn't understand what made me feel sad and reluctant to see him leave. I had other professors. Why didn't I have enthusiasm for them? Perhaps they were not easy to approach, not warm-hearted, frank and willing to help people wholeheartedly like my professor. For example, a professor who had the same name as the famous philosopher Hegel didn't know how to respect others. If a student made a mistake in his class he would excitedly repeat it, making the student feel uncomfortable for days.

Anyway I was very upset that he was leaving. In those six months I had enjoyed his encouragement and learned a lot about the history of literature. I had planned to take another course from him next semester. I had also decided to see him after I finished my paper and invite him to have a real Chinese dinner at my dorm before the coming vacation. I still kept a piece of silk in my suitcase and waited to give it to his wife as a gift when he invited me to his home. But now all my plans vanished like soap bubbles. That whole night I let my imagination run away with me. I turned on the television and radio. Actually I was not listening to them; I just wanted to make some noise to divert my attention. I tossed about in bed until midnight before I finally got to sleep.

The next day was Friday. I carried my Chinese dish to the department library where the farewell party was going to be held. Many students had arrived earlier and brought all kinds of food. Seeing me, my professor walked over to say hello. I said nothing, but quietly helped him to put all the food on the tables. Then I found a chair in a corner and sat down. I didn't want to disturb him again on this unusual occasion because I knew he would be the busiest person at the party. So I started a conversation with a teaching assistant sitting beside me.

"Don't you know that his leave meant he would lose the job?" the assistant said.

I was startled. I didn't believe such ill fortune was awaiting him. My head hummed and my eyes filled with tears. How could such a young and well-qualified professor lose his job? I couldn't accept this fact. Seeing my puzzled look he explained the details to me from beginning to end.

My professor had passed the state examination qualifying him to teach as a professor but could not find a job in a university. Just at that time, however, a professor in the Literature Department was going to work in Africa for three years so my professor temporarily got the job. Now the other professor was coming back home to take up his old position.

"But he can be a lecturer then," I said. "There are

a lot of lifelong lecturers in the department."

"Impossible," the assistant smiled and said, "because he has received the qualification of a professor. No school can employ a professor to teach as a lecturer. His standard is high so he should earn more money. If he is employed as a lecturer, isn't that wasting his abilities?"

Upon hearing his words I could not remain calm anymore. Actually, I was even more confused. Was it not considered a waste to let a qualified professor stay at home doing nothing? I can understand that posts for lifelong professors are very limited because lifelong professors have a lot of priviliges even after they retire. In this case, why couldn't a college or university have more lecturers?

I was really shocked. It was the first time that I heard a professor could also lose his job in Germany. Now everything was suddenly clear to me why my professor did not drive to work, why he always wore that same dark gray clothes and why he did not go to lunch at the dinning hall, but enjoyed nibbling his dried bread brought from home.

"Will any other college or university employ him after he returns home?" I stared at the assistant and asked.

"There are few chances for him according to the present economic situation and besides, he is engaged in written literature," he replied.

"How will he live?"

"He has to depend on his wife, or earn some money by writing books, or draw unemployment insurance from the government."

I was dumbstruck and my heart sank. I imagined what a miserable life he would have and wondered whether he would live in poverty or commit suicide. I didn't want to continue to think deeply but my thoughts lingered on and strung together all the tragic scenes I once read in novels, watched and heard on television. I lifted my head and looked at my professor. He was sitting in a chair beside the door looking solemn. His usual complacent expression in class had disappeared. His face was getting obviously thinner and a dark shadow came to his eyes. Only his moustache stuck up higher than before. I suddenly walked to him bravely, giving a sad cry: "Professor!" I was feeling choked up and could not utter another word. He held me in his arms and patted me on the back, saying: "Don't worry. Everything will be all right."

Just at that moment the chairman of our department arrived, followed by a group of professors and lecturers. At once the quiet atmosphere was broken. People greeted each other and talked warmly.

The chairman of the department first said a few words, then my professor made a speech: "It's against my will to leave here." As he finished this sentence, some girls, who were more sentimental than I, started crying. I, too, was feeling very sad and didn't hear what he said afterwards, but only caught that he had left his address on the door of the library and he welcomed everyone to write him.

The atmosphere that night was oppressive throughout the party. A few minutes after my professor's speech the chairman said that he had other things to do and left the room. Soon some professors and lecturers also made excuses and bid good-bye to my professor.

At that moment many students were sitting around talking with the professor. That night he acted differently. He was very active and talkative. Sometimes he cracked jokes and he looked happy and relaxed. For three years he was worrying that his job would be taken away. Now he didn't have to worry any more. He was free and would be happy to budget his own time to do what he liked. However, I saw that a little sadness flashed in his eyes when he stopped talking.

A soft melody came out from a tape recorder. Nobody danced, but sat at tables drinking and eating quietly. Even those who were chatting lowered their voices. Everyone was afraid to ruin this solemn atmosphere and make the professor unhappy.

Night thickened. Students still remained in their chairs talking. It seemed that they had no intention of leaving. Unfortunately I had to go before them because I would set off early the next morning to visit a good friend living in Lubeck, a city about 200 kilometres away. I wanted to say good-bye to the professor before I stepped out of the room, but seeing he was talking enthusiastically with students of our class, I did not have the heart to interrupt him. I left silently.

That was a mistake. On the Monday after the party, I found that the little paper that had the professor's address and telephone number had disappeared. I asked every person on duty in the library but all of them said they didn't know about it because they were not on duty that weekend. I got angry and immediately ran to the Language Department library and then to the bulletin board. It would not be there but I didn't want to give up until I saw all the doors of professors' offices. The little paper must have been taken away by someone. I suddenly felt hopeless and my legs felt like jelly. I dragged myself to the emergency exit of the building and sat right on the spot. I did not expect this would happen. If only I had written them down when I left there on Friday. But who could I ask for it? The summer vacation was approaching. We would not have examinations this semester. I guessed most of my classmates were busy preparing to go home and I had little chance of running into someone. But I still wanted to try my luck and kept going to the department every day for a few weeks. I failed at last. I despaired and regretted having left the party in a hurry. I had no other alternative but to wait for the new semester.

After that, whenever I heard the telephone ring in the corridor, I hoped that it was from the professor. I had to control myself from going to answer the phone. Sometimes, when I heard footsteps coming towards my room, my heart would beat so fast it felt as if it would jump out of my throat. But if the footsteps went past my room and the call was not for me, I would turn away sullenly to my room from the door. I thought I couldn't go on tormenting myself any more. I began to invite friends to my room on weekends. We talked and laughed. Only then did time seem to pass quickly. But no matter what I did, I never left my room. I was afraid the professor would call me at any moment. If once he called and I was not in, how disappointed he would be! One day one of my friends persuaded me to go to "The Magic Flute," an opera I had longed to see for a long time. I turned it over in my mind again and again and finally decided reluctantly to give up the chance.

A few days later I received a letter from home which moved up my return date. I started running around booking my air ticket, packing up, and buying souvenirs for friends. It took me about a month to get everything ready.

I was rushed on the day of my departure. All my friends came to say good-bye, but I seemed to be waiting for someone else. It was my professor, whom I wanted to see and talk to. I didn't know why he didn't call me. He might remember my telephone number. Perhaps he did not want to recall the past, perhaps he was busy all day looking for a job or perhaps he had already forgotten me. That last thought made me cry; I didn't believe he could forget me. He must feel some unutterable bitterness he did not want to reveal to anyone who knew him well. Perhaps he was too busy those days. I'm sure he will call me when he has time.

I turned to my friends and urged them again to put my home address on the wall beside the telephone so that he would know I had left Germany for home.

When the large aircraft took off in the dusk, I didn't draw my face close to the window like other passengers to have a last look at Frankfurt ablaze with lights. I remained in my seat with my eyes closed. I silently said good-bye to the country where I had spent six months and wished my professor and friends good luck in finding jobs in the future.

The plane carried me with my regrets and best wishes, gradually flying farther and farther away from the city, which soon vanished in the evening haze.

The Winter Is Also Warm

Ni Wa

W E stayed in an old man's house when we visited Oslo, the capital of Norway.

When summer comes, hotels in northern European countries are often fully booked for the season. So the Travel Promotion Bureau encourages local people to rent out any extra rooms they might have to travellers. Not only does this provide local people with an additional source of income, but it is also of benefit to the tourist industry. Thus we were able to stay with this elderly Norwegian man.

Billy, who was in his seventies, lived alone in a seven-room building in the suburbs; he was tall and robust but what I admired most about his appearance was his thick, shiny silver hair, which conveyed the impression of intelligence and depth rather than infirmity and old age. Billy ushered us upstairs into our room. The bed was well padded and comfortable; the other furniture was old and very elegant. On the bedside table was a vase with fresh flowers from the garden. The whole room was filled with a soft fragrance. Spacious and clean, it still only cost a little more than 30 Singapore dollars each day!

It was raining. After taking a bath we lay in bed reading the tourist literature we had picked up earlier. We planned to stay in until the rain stopped. Then there was a knock on the door. In came Billy, smiling. He asked politely: "Would you like to have a cup of coffee in the living room? It is so cold outside. Coffee'll warm you up." The living room was full of the thick aroma of coffee. On the shelf were many framed photographs of children, probably his grandchildren. But the one that attracted me most was the large colour photo in the centre. Although the woman in the picture was obviously not young, there was an indescribable charm in her features, particularly her eyebrows and lips. Seeing how transfixed I had become looking at that photograph, the old man smiled:

"She was my wife."

After a short pause, he added:

"She died of cancer ten years ago."

"Then you live alone now?"

"Yes. My children have all grown up and flown away. It is naturally the old bird who guards the nest." I could tell that, having experienced many of the vicissitudes of life, he had come to a deeper understanding of the meaning of life. His three sons all lived outside Oslo. The eldest one was a newspaper correspondent in Bergen, the second a manager in a Swedish corporation who lived in Stockholm, and the youngest a businessman who spent most of his time abroad. Was he lonely without his children?

"Lonely?" he asked, staring at me with his bright

eyes. "Nothing of the kind! I don't even know what loneliness is. To be honest, I haven't ever enjoyed myself so much as now that my children have grown up and I am retired. It is a luxury to have all your time free. Every day I listen to music, read books, plant flowers and study a foreign language. I often feel time is too limited. Sometimes I would like to ski in the mountains or swim in the ocean."

Oh, how rare it is to see a person of his age this happy! Most people believe that age is the life killer and that one's activities are always constrained by it. But the brave old man in front of me had been able to conquer the killer and was now enjoying all the things that the old usually were deprived of. As though he could read the thoughts that had been racing through my mind, the old man continued to talk on the subject after he had taken a few gulps of coffee.

"Everyone can have a meaningful and happy life if he lives. I decided not to let myself plunge into gloom any longer after I died once."

"Died?" I was surprised and said, "Have you been seriously ill before?"

"Yes, very seriously." His voice was filled up with the sadness he had experienced a long time ago. Pointing to his chest, he said, "But it was not a physical disease. Something was wrong with my heart."

"Heart disease, then?"

He shook his head.

"The year when my wife died of cancer was our fortieth anniversary. In the three years during which she was confined to bed, I kept on hoping that a miracle would happen. But she passed away at last. While she was dying, she kept calling out my name. In my mind I can still see the look that was on her face."

Losing one's wife when one is old is indeed one of the saddest experiences in life. Feeling deep sympathy for him, I listened to him quietly.

"I felt I died with her. I had been spiritually destroyed. Later on, with psychiatric treatment that lasted a little over twelve months, I gradually got used to life without her. I understand now that God has left me alone in the world, I should enjoy fully the time that I have left before I meet her again in Heaven."

After this personal tragedy, the old man finally managed to sail his boat into a calm harbour, where it was warm but not hot in summer, and cool but not cold in winter. Here the old man was spending the rest of his life.

The Finnish Girl

Yang Erlin

A few months had passed since I arrived in Helsinki, capital of Finland. Though by now I could offer my own views about Helsinki after adapting myself to the city, I always felt something wanting. Having returned this time from the countryside, I realized I lacked a deep understanding of the Finnish people and Finnish culture. As an overseas Chinese student, I lived in Finland as if I were in the Land of Peach Blossom which was totally cut off from outside, "turning a deaf ear to the current affairs, only devoting myself to the books of saints."

I began to know Pavi after being introduced to my colleague in the lab. The first time I met her in the great dinning hall of the main building in the University of Helsinki she reminded me of the girls from the countryside in China who crowd into Beijing to make a living. Pavi had left home for Helsinki after she graduated from high school at 19. Now she was a senior student in the university. The flourishing noisy city hadn't yet changed this country girl's pure and honest character. I immediately noticed her sincerity and warmth. When she knew I was Chinese, she said: "It is not very often one can get acquainted with a Chinese friend. Your country has such a long history of civilization while Finland only has a history of less than 100 years." That made me think. With so short a history, Finland has developed its economy rapidly and its living standard has risen to such a high level that it stands among the developed countries in the world. China, with a long history, has fallen behind for various reasons in many fields.

"I must go to China someday," she said when we parted.

"China is a beautiful oriental country with a culture different from the Western culture. You will find it is worth visiting," I said.

She left a deep impression on me although I had met her only once. Pavi was not a good-looking girl from her people's point of view. But her large, pretty and thoughtful eyes and modest, humorous way of talking produced a charm no one could deny. This characteristic distinguished her from the city girls who were famous for their bold and unrestrained manners. So I was pleased to accept her invitation to visit her home in the countryside.

The Finnish countryside in June was wonderful. Green fields alternated with stretches of forest with beautiful farm houses like stars embellishing the sky. Blue limpid lakes glimmered like the scales of fish in the sun. Sitting in the car, I enjoyed the captivating scenery. Pavi drove the car she had borrowed from her father to meet me at the station. She had learned to drive five years ago, but she got few chances to drive at the university and felt a little rusty. However, now she was driving at 140 kilometres per hour on the country road.

We soon pulled up in front of some farm houses. I couldn't believe my eyes that it was Pavi's home. I was warmly received by her parents at the door. Since Pavi was the only daughter in her family, I thought, she must be pampered.

The sound "moo" suddenly attracted my attention. There was a herd of plump, sturdy, pied cows eating grass. Calves were playing around their mothers, such a natural, harmonious scene.

Pavi looked at her watch: "You need to have a good rest. It's time for me to milk the cows." "What? You such a weak girl can do that kind of work?" I followed her to the cowshed. The cows were driven to their own places just as students run to their seats when the bell rings. Ten big cows stood in a line while the five calves frolicked in the next cowshed. Pavi first cleaned the udder of the cow, then connected the small milking machine to the four huge nipples. In order to keep the cow from giving a backward kick, she clipped round-headed iron hook to its thigh as well as its backbone. Everyone knew how stubborn a cow could be if it lost its temper. With the rhythmic sound of the machine, the cow's full, plump udders gradually shrank. Every time Pavi finished milking a cow, she would pat it on the back, murmuring a few words of praise. And the cow, in response, would moo and swish its tail. I couldn't help exclaiming with admiration when Pavi started the machine. It was beyond my imagination that a cow can produce so much milk.

Pavi told me: "A good cow can produce 15 litres of milk each time. We milk them twice a day, in the morning and in the afternoon." The famous poem by Lu Xun at that time came across my mind: "Fierce-browed, I coolly defy a thousand pointing fingers; head-bowed, like a willing cow I serve the children." Now I understood the real meaning of the willing cow who served the children. I gazed at Pavi, who was holding the plump udder with one hand and managing the milking machine with the other. As the cows left manure, Pavi had to spread straw in the cowshed to dry the ground. The mixed smell filling the air made me sick and dizzy, but Pavi was happy and relaxed with her work, as she put it: "How can I feel unhappy with my friends?" It surprised me that Pavi, the university student could bear hardship like that. After Pavi had milked the cow, she poured the milk into the storage tank where it was collected by the dairy every two days.

Drinking fresh milk at the table, I could not but admire Pavi. She smiled: "This is nothing. I come back home to help my parents during summer vacation. Thus they will have a month's rest. It is not easy for them to work hard all year." These words gave me another shock. At home, I had been told often that Western people's sense of family was being dulled, that people refused to have anything to do with relatives and friends. There were no dutiful children any more. But now before me stood a filial daughter. "Finland has a sparse population, especially in the countryside," Pavi said. "As there is a long distance between each farming house, people within one family cherish a deep affection for each other. I really don't know how to express my love for my parents." I noticed her parents gazing with deep feeling at her, full of love and pride.

Evening came, Pavi sat in front of the piano and from her hands emerged clear and melodious music, making the tranquil night in the countryside even more beautiful. Pavi began to learn to play the piano at 12. She told me that once in her childhood she was a guest at her uncle's with her parents, she heard sweet music coming from the neighbourhood when she was playing outside in the snow. She followed the music to find a girl her age was playing the piano. Pavi was so absorbed in watching the girl's playing that she forgot everything. Her absence caused worry at her uncle's because nobody knew where she had gone. When they found her and before her parents had time to get angry, she asked to learn to play the piano. From then on, the sound of the piano became part of her family's life. Listening to her play, her parents melted a day's tiredness into satisfying smiles. Particularly during the long and cold winter in Finland, the music played on the piano seemed even more important. Thus Pavi, nurtured in music, had grown into an accomplished young woman.

Pavi had confidence in her future. Though she was born and brought up in the countryside and had a deep feeling for her hometown, she still hoped to open up a new world in the capital. The first time she went to Helsinki, she had great difficulties as a girl with no one to turn to. She had to find a job to earn some money to cover her expenses from last term. She had a hard time in winter because of the cold weather. The intense competition of work and life in the capital called for a strong will and adaptability. From Pavi I could see the resolution, tenacity, patience and self-confidence that characterize the Finnish people.

When I left her home, Pavi said smiling: "You have told me that your country is now carrying out a birth control programme, and every couple can have only one child, so a great number of single sons and daughters have become the 'little emperors' of the family. What are you going to do with your child?" Her question was quite beyond my expectation. The film "The Last Emperor" about the story of Pu Yi -- the last emperor of China -- had been shown in Finland for almost two months. Pavi surely understood what the "little emperor" meant. The traditional Chinese way of bringing up children in the family should be changed. In Finland, it was society, not the family, that influenced the children. Children learned young to face the real society they would enter as adults. They were given the independence to compete as individuals in the society, which in an advanced country with a highly developed commodity economy was of great importance. Compared with Pavi, I understood that what children brought up in the Chinese family lacked was exactly that sense of competition. They were weak in will, slack in spirit and common in quality. Pavi told me her parents gave her a small amount of money every month in order to cultivate a sense of financial independence. They often made suggestions about how she should spend her money and what she should buy. But Pavi was the person who had the final say. Her parents respected her choices. With such experience, she learned the value and importance of money in society and could probe deeply into the outside world. Different from Pavi's parents, parents in China have strict control of their children's money. They decide everything. While not ignoring China's economic reality, I have to say that this incorrect attitude has meant that Chinese children know little about today's economy. Only slowly do they develop their sense of social responsibility.

I smiled in reply: "I hope when you meet my child in China you won't be disappointed."

II. North America

Miscellaneous Talks on the People of the East and West

Liu Yung Ho

O RIENTALS and Westerners differ greatly in their historical and cultural backgrounds, national characters, ethics, and social customs and habits. In the past, most Chinese impressions of Western people were shaped by the reports of Chinese students and diplomats returned from abroad. But their reports were often lopsided and limited, given the fact that students' lives were usually confined to campuses and diplomats hardly mingled with the common people. In addition, the ingrained Chinese tradition of glossing over the negative and praising the positive would inevitably render an inaccurate picture of Westerners in the minds of many Chinese. But reason tells us that no people, whether in the East or West, can be seen as inferior, nor be free of faults.

On the other hand, some Westerners still have prejudice and discriminate against the Chinese as they had in the past. Many Western tourists come to China only to photograph such novelties as the bound feet of older women, the split pants of the children and bamboo strips used as toilet paper. They see the Great Wall as a mysterious emblem of this Far Eastern country, overlooking the spirit of steadfastness it represents. They take no interest in modern Chinese architectural masterpieces like the Yangtze River Bridge in Nanjing and the Gezhouba Dam, as there are also such projects in their own countries. There is no evidence to assert that they come to China just to pick faults, but most of the stories of the Western mass media about China tell of its backward side.

If we want to obtain a deeper understanding of Westerners, we must not overlook how Westerners view China. I myself have lived in Toronto, Canada, for 20 years. The following account, based on my personal experience there, lists some major differences between the Western people and the Chinese, which may serve as your reference.

Customs and Habits Are Poles Apart

The different customs and habits in China and the West sometimes make mutual understanding difficult. To Chinese eyes, some Western customs are understandable but others seem ridiculous.

When Chinese people get married, the wedding ceremony and feast are always held in the bridegroom's home. But in the West, it is usually the duty of the bride's family to arrange the wedding. Once I received an invitation which begins with the following, "Ms XX, daughter of Mr. and Mrs. XX, requests the pleasure of Mr. Yung Ho Liu at her wedding ceremony...." Actually I didn't know Mr. and Mrs. XX, the senders of the invitation, or the bride herself. But when I continued to read, I saw that the groom was the son of a friend of mine and realized it was the bride's family that took care of the wedding preparations. This custom would actually mean a loss of face to many Chinese. Another friend of mine felt uncomfortable when he saw his son's wedding ceremony hosted by the bride's family, and his arrogance dampened the whole atmosphere.

To show intimacy, Westerners of all ages, even between young and old people, prefer to call people by their first names. For example, Mr. Wang Dahua once went to another city to visit his son's family. When he arrived, his foreign daughter-in-law greeted him by saying, "Hello, Mr. Wang. Welcome you to our home. How is Mrs. Wang? Why isn't she here with you?" A few days later, she simply called him by his first name to shorten the social distance: "Would you like one more cup of coffee, Dahua?" For most Chinese, this way of using names means a lack of respect and is unacceptable.

The Chinese have a saying, "Dutiful children are educated by club." They believe that children must be strictly disciplined from childhood, and beating is an indispensable part of their education. Never do that in the West or before Westerners. You will be accused of child abuse and put into jail if the children are found to have bruises. To make things worse, the government could entrust your children to the care of other families on the grounds that you are not a qualified father or mother. But it is ridiculous that Chinese parents not be free to bring up their children in their own rigorous way.

In the West, suckling babies in public is considered impolite and even against the law, which is unthinkable to the Chinese. Is it because that Westerners are more conservative and feudal-minded than us? Of course not. It is not against the law that, in the heat of summer, women can wander about in city streets, on beaches and at parks wearing low-cut tops and even bikinis. It is not against the law either that bar girls can give dancing performances at night with nothing on. But they think it rude that mothers breast-feed their babies in public. How funny!

The Difference in Human Touch

In a Western country, if you are a stranger and lose your way, choose anyone on the street for help. Most probably, he will stop and answer your questions as to where the post office is, where you can find a telephone, etc. If he doesn't know the place you want, he will also make a point of helping you by asking other passers-by.

But what I encountered during a visit to relatives back home in 1982 was quite another story. One day in Beijing, while looking from the window at one of my friends' home, I saw there were several telephone sets in an office across the street. I walked over there and asked the three people sitting there: "Excuse me, can I use your phone please?" Without lifting their heads, they blurted out almost in unison, "No." Then I asked, "Where can I find a public telephone?" The answer was "Don't know." But only minutes later, I found a telephone in a small shop just on the other side of the street. More than 20 years had elapsed since I emigrated to Canada, but the bad Chinese habit of treating strangers with frosty looks remained unchanged. No wonder on July 18, 1988 *People's Daily* (overseas edition) carried a report on asking for directions in Guangzhou. Foreigners would laugh their heads off at that because asking the way has never been considered worthy of a news story in their countries.

Whether at home or abroad, the Chinese need to be more tender-hearted towards strangers. One day in a Toronto park my friend and I met an old overseas Chinese who was neatly dressed and looked well educated. My friend went up to him and began the conversation: "You came here alone, Old Man? It's wonderful to go to park in such a nice weather." To our surprise, the old man got angry and said, "I don't know you. Why do you talk to me?" How strange that a man of such maturity and experience had no human feelings. If he were a Western elder, he would most likely make some room for you to sit down on the bench and start chatting away with you about this and that. At least, he would respond with a few polite words.

But why do Westerners who have been to China think that the Chinese are friendly and warm-hearted? Yes, they are. But their warmth depends on to whom it is extended. No matter where they are, at home or abroad, the Chinese are warm-hearted only to foreigners, but not to their fellow countrymen, only to the people they know, but not to strangers.

I am not faulting my Chinese compatriots. But I really believe that we Chinese should learn from our Western friends in this regard. Their hospitality does not discriminate between countrymen and foreigners, between relatives and strangers.

Government Officials in the West Are Genuine Servants of the People

As the name implies, public servants in Western countries, called "cadres" in China, serve the people in earnest. Almost all the public servants I dealt with were polite and helpful. The Chinese have a saying, "The biggest fear of the rank and file is not official control, but officials themselves." In China, even the lowest officeholders can make you into a docile horse. On this point, Western officialdom really is worth praising.

I remember at the customs office more than twenty years ago when we emigrated to Canada. An emigration officer smilingly asked me if I spoke English or French. After he knew that I could speak some English, he said, "Good. Welcome to live in Canada!" Then he examined my credentials and gave me a form to fill in. He showed me how to complete the form and even corrected errors for me. Finally he said, "I hope you like Canada and have good luck." I really felt flattered as I had never seen such a polite official so lacking in bureaucratic airs.

Immigrants were asked to find jobs in a personnel centre. After registration, I was interviewed by an amiable, middle-aged woman. Many days passed, but I still got no answer. I had to go and inquire about it. The woman received me again. I said, "Excuse me. I've come to see if there is any opportunity here." She smiled and said, "Don't feel sorry. I'm very glad you are here. Just imagine. Without you immigrants seeking jobs, I would lose my job myself. I'll let you know as soon as I find a vacancy. You can wait at home and don't need to come in such cold weather." The Chinese would understand her words as a euphemism telling me not to come any more or that I had very little chance. To my surprise, on the afternoon of the third day, she called to tell me that the Department of Food Science at the University of Toronto was looking for a chemical technician. If I wanted to have a try, she could notify the dean to give me an interview next morning. It never occurred to me then that I would do the job right until my retirement.

Whatever you apply for from the government — a low rent house, pension or medical insurance — the people who receive you are always polite, amiable and helpful. I have never seen anyone deliberately make things difficult.

When I was back in the motherland, I could see the slogan "Serve the People" everywhere. But from airliner stewardesses to shop assistants, I could not find an example of serving the people wholeheartedly. Almost all of them put on a stern expression. Once in Beijing I went into a drugstore. The woman who served me was very pretty, but her cold face really disgusted me. In the manner of a father lecturing his child, I said to her, "You don't know how pretty you are when you smile. Don't you feel tired to put on such a face all day long?" She made no response.

We should admire and copy attitude of the Western public servants in serving the people. China should not only send students abroad to study advanced science and technology of the West, but also government officials to learn from their Western counterparts about service with a smile.

Strike — A Thing as Horrible as Tigers for Chinese

In the West, strikes are the workers' means of demanding wage increases from capitalists. But the present capitalists have become clever enough to hike prices soon after they satisfy the workers' demands, thereby shifting the cost to consumers. Thus strikes are often seen as a powerful weapon in the hands of the unions. Postal officers get more pay after they go on a strike. But who would be willing to lag behind? Other groups such as automobile workers and public transportation workers soon follow suit. Consequently, reports on strikes flood newspapers all year round.

To enhance the threatening aspect of strikes, labour unions often call them at critical times of the year. Airline employees and public transportation workers tend to call strikes immediately before significant holidays; post office workers go on strike at the end of the year when people are busy sending Christmas cards; teachers go on strike before a new term starts. Everyone has the right to strike. But it would be incredible to Chinese that teachers, often esteemed as paragons of virtue and learning, could leave their students behind in class for a few more dollars, and that doctors could ignore their patients' sufferings and lives for a wage increase. Once, policemen in Montreal went on a strike, leaving the city in disorder. Immediately after sunset, some young hooligans broke into shops and looted everything in sight. After a night of commotion, the busiest sections of the city were a mess.

I myself fear public transportation strikes the most, for they make my outdoor activities very difficult. I remember that, in a strike by Toronto bus drivers, people had to drive their cars to work and pick up those who had no vehicles. Thousands of private cars thronged the streets and no one could move an inch. Viewed from above, the whole city looked like a giant, spectacular parking lot. I also didn't like the strikes by postal workers, which cut off my information from newspapers, magazines and letters.

In the free world, everybody is free to go on a strike and everybody has to pay a price for it.

To a typical Chinese like me, Westerners are skilled in threatening each other at critical moments regardless of the interests of people, who have no alternative.

Public Health: Acute Diseases Are Often Cured by Slow Doctors

Patients with slight illnesses like a cold often go to see family doctors in the United States and Canada, doctors who have a broad, but superficial medical knowledge. Clinics are scattered in residential areas.

According to statistics from the Canadian and American medical associations, the average family doctor is responsible for the care of 600 to 900 households. Clinics are often crowded with patients who line up outside and wait their turn. They must phone the doctor to make an appointment beforehand, otherwise they will not be received. When patients suffer from specific or serious diseases, they will be transferred to the care of specialists who are even fewer in number. Patients often have to wait ten or more days and sometimes even months for treatment. People would ask why Westerners are so slow in medical treatment. Aren't they famous for working efficiency? As everyone knows, they certainly value efficiency very much, but only efficiency in making money. Small wonder their efficiency in medical treatment is lowered. Western doctors practise medicine only to make money. When they treat patients, they are doing business.

Doctors in the West seem to regard their patients as out-of-order cars waiting to be fixed. They make a diagnosis only according to the results of chemical examinations and physical check-ups. If an examination report shows everything is normal, the doctor will conclude the patient is healthy without considering whether there are illnesses medical devices cannot detect. Even if the patient claims to feel very bad, the doctor will refuse to prescribe medicine for him. But when the symptom becomes apparent to all, the disease is too serious to be cured. To the Chinese this is unacceptable medical practice and not in keeping with the spirit of Hippocrates.

In Canada, medical insurance is generally provided by the government. Each family only needs to pay 400 to 500 Canadian dollars a year for comprehensive insurance that includes hospitalization, operations and even obstetrics. The situation is different in the United States where private companies undertake the responsibility for personal health insurance. The insurance only covers a fee range from 1,000 to 50,000 U.S. dollars. Patients have to pay for medical treatments below $1,000 and above $50,000. You cannot afford to get a serious disease in the United States as it will eat up most of your money. Hospitalization alone can cost several hundred dollars a day, and operations can cost thousands of dollars. In the United States, the elderly have preferential medical treatment, but that only lasts ten days. Beyond that period, no further free care is given regardless of their condition.

Canada has one of the best medical systems among the economically advanced countries. All people, poor or rich, old or young, enjoy the opportunity to have good medical care. Those above the age of 65 receive medical treatment without paying. In the States, if a poor person gets seriously ill, he will have problems.

Dealing with Westerners

Westerners are noted for efficiency in working. In business negotiations, they speak in concise, curt and to-the-point language. Eloquent and thoughtful, Western traders are well-bred for doing business. For them, doing business talk is an art that enables you to grab what you need from the other party with the latter's agreement.

Books and tape cassettes on negotiation skills are available in Western countries. The Chinese, however, are poorly trained in this regard. Small wonder that we Chinese swallowed many losses in both foreign affairs and business negotiations.

The following is an example of my contacts with Westerners, from which we can see that they sometimes are not so easy-going as imagined.

One day, my wife and I were shopping in a supermarket and we paid $1.50 for a purchase. My wife handed over a five-dollar bill to the salesgirl, but she only gave change of several cents. After my wife told her the mistake, the girl insisted that my wife had only paid $2, which angered me so much that I had to take the field. I went to reason with her, but she simply cut me dead as though there were nobody before her eyes. I had never seen a person of such overweening arrogance. In despair, I asked, "Where is the manager?" After a while, a

young man came out from the backroom and rude-
ly said to me, "Why are you shouting here?" "She
didn't give me the right change," I said, " and simply
ignored me when I told her. How would you have
come out if I hadn't called out loudly?"

He said, "You said you paid $5, but she said she
only got two. There is no evidence to prove who is
right and who is wrong." I told him the mistake
would come to light if we checked all the receipts
against the total cash. "But how can we let such a
long shopping queue wait for that long?" he asked.
I said, "No. Now that she had made a mistake, she
could make it again. Are you sure you can check it
out in the end?" Unexpectedly, he pointed his finger
at me and shouted, "Did you ever make a mistake
before? No one can be immune to faults."

This has become a pet phrase of Westerners, one
that may stop you if you are not prepared for it. I
said, "Yes, you are right. But remember she is working now and no mistakes can be pardoned at this
moment. If the girl hands you an account after work
missing $50 and says 'no one can be immune to
faults,' will you let her go?" He didn't expect that an
old Chinese, who spoke poor English, could de-
nounce him down to the last point. He changed his
face and patted me on the shoulder, saying, "Trust
me please. I'll check up, at least to maintain the
company's reputation." The next morning, he told
me on the phone that there turned out to be an
extra $3 in yesterday's accounts and asked me to
come and get them. Here you can see how difficult
it is to deal with Westerners.

Absurd Punishment of Crimes

Big cities in the eastern United States such as New York, Chicago and Detroit each witness over 1,000 murders a year. In Toronto, where I live, there are an average of 50 or so homicides each year. Though the crime rate in Canada pales compared to the American rate, it still seems amazingly high to a Chinese.

Nearly half of the murders are rooted in family disputes, which often lead to killings between fathers and sons, husbands and wives and of the whole family by the father who kills himself thereafter. Property-related murders are few and far between, but many women are killed after being raped to prevent them from making an accusation. If a rapist of a 14-year-old girl is identified, he will be given an prison term of 20 years. But if he kills the girl, he may escape scot-free. If by any chance he is caught later, he may still hope to be released on bail after several years in jail, even though he has been sentenced to life-imprisonment. In my opinion, the problem here is the law itself, which sometimes seems to encourage murder. Teenage boys and girls have little hope of returning alive once they have disappeared; their bodies are usually found in the wilderness.

Several years ago, a dozen girls disappeared one after another in western Canada. Justice has a long arm. The murderer was caught red-handed at last. When asked by the police if he was responsible for the other cases of child abuse and murder, he denied it at first, but later demanded a hefty sum as a requirement for his confession. Eager to wind up the long-unsolved case, the police had to consent. Then he led the police to where he had hidden the girls' bodies. After that, the criminal went so far as to declare that he would like to write in detail about how and why he had molested and killed these girls if someone offered him a handsome price, say, half a million dollars. Some publishers expressed interest until their fear of public opinion made them back down.

Another story is also worth mentioning here. A husband pulled out a handgun and pointed it at his wife when the couple fell into a terrible quarrel. After the other family members failed to stop him, they called the police. When the police arrived, the husband killed one of the policemen and was arrested on the spot. Many people regarded such a man as a scourage of the society and thought there was no reason for him to live. But many also held a sit-in demonstration in front of the jail to oppose his execution. What is more incredible to the Chinese is that the deceased policeman's wife was also among the demonstrators.

In North America, most killings are done on impulse, and not necessarily out of deep hatred. The young man who shot President Reagan was trying to win the attention of a movie actress he loved. Although the man he tried to kill was the president, he was sent to a psychiatric hospital for treatment after doctors proved he suffered from a mental disorder. This is also incredible to the Chinese people. Westerners believe that murdering is an abnormal activity, which would never be done by normal people. From this, they conclude that murderers are abnormal people and that abnormal people should be regarded as patients and patients should be cared for and cured, not punished. If the murderer fails to kill the man, that is fine of course. If he does kill him, as the man is already dead, what reason do we have to destroy another life? Capital punishment, they say, may not necessarily stop killing among mentally ill people. And if judges give improperly severe penalties, it is they who are really committing a crime.

All these arguments sound like absolute nonsense to the Chinese, who hold it as an unalterable principle that a murderer must pay with his life. But Westerners think it is inhuman to execute murderers, rapists and criminals. Chinese and Westerners have little common ground on this point. To us, the punishment of crime in the West is absurd.

She Loves Man,
But Not Men

Yuan Honggeng

OWING to the nature of my trade — a university teacher of English — I have gotten to know many Western people. As the Chinese saying goes, "People are varied if there are many." The Americans, Englishmen, Australians and Canadians I have met were all different from one another; so were their attitudes towards the Chinese people around them.

Some of them liked, or even loved, both China and the Chinese, while some preferred the former, some the latter. Although most Occidentals staying in China would declare they were friends of the local people, some foreign attitudes came as a surprise, even a shock. Few showed their dislike, contempt, or even disgust so plainly as to put themselves in hostile surroundings, but their real feelings could be easily detected.

Marie, a Canadian girl, whose full name I won't mention here, belonged to this lot.

She was young and quite pretty by both oriental and occidental standards, so she drew people's attention and won their favour as soon as she arrived at the school as an English teacher. Being a Canadian, she could skate gracefully. On the school's small, round artificial ice rink, in her red coat, she was like a flying angel in the Dunhuang Grottoes. Her performance on the ice increased her charm; people on the campus were fascinated by this foreign beauty. They showed their liking in many ways — smiling at her, waving to her on the way, inviting her to come to the front of a milk-queue....

It was beyond doubt that she was proud. But weren't most pretty young girls proud, including Chinese girls? Besides, hadn't she declared she loved China and its people wholeheartedly? Hadn't she enjoyed *jiaozi*, laughed at a Chinese anecdote, and burst into tears when Japanese soldiers tore open a child's belly on TV? Those Chinese who could speak English would say hello to her when they met her. She was also quite friendly towards the people around her. Thus, as a colleague of Marie, I enjoyed this "Sino-Canadian friendship" as others did, until something very unpleasant happened.

One winter evening, when it was very cold outside, I went skating. As usual, I saw Marie there, together with Johnson, an American professor of chemistry. She was making one small spiral after another in the centre of the rink, arms behind her back, legs swinging beautifully, with her friend following closely behind. After a while, she saw me and waved. I made a similar gesture; conversation was impossible because there were so many people around.

I was a beginner in the sport so I kept to the

edge, awkwardly dragging my body in all directions, avoiding the rushing stream of skaters. Suddenly a big thump came from somewhere on the ice and the skaters milled around in confusion. Peeping through many moving legs, I saw a young boy sprawled in the centre of the rink. "Blood! He is hurt," someone shouted in panic.

When I scrambled to the spot, the American professor and two Chinese students, having already darted to the boy's side, were trying to lift him off the ice. About 10 yards away, a man was dragging a stretcher to the blood-stained spot. Marie, sitting on her fur-lined gloves, cool as a cucumber, was examining her skates, which were bent slightly. The boy was carried away immediately to the school clinic. The crowd thinned out but a few remaining people stared angrily at Marie. I also looked at the two foreigners. Catching my questioning eyes, Johnson explained what had happened. The boy had been sitting in the very centre of the rink, fastening his skates, while Marie narrowed her circles before abruptly making a quick turn, cutting the boy's left shin with one of her skates.

"Let her pay for the medical care!" someone snarled.

"Why didn't you even apologize?" I asked.

At first Marie didn't hear me, or pretended she didn't, then she stared at me blankly, put on her shoes, got up, gathered her things and walked away in the direction of her apartment.

We were all puzzled and watched her dim figure until it vanished in the woods in front of the auditorium.

"Maybe she just feels awful and doesn't feel like talking," Johnson conjectured after a long silence.

The next day I bumped into Marie in the reference room. She greeted me with an "Hi" and came over to discuss a movie she had seen, saying how much she liked it. Obviously she didn't want to talk about the injured boy and the accident.

Several days later, I met her again in the dining hall.

"Don't you want to know what had happened to that boy?" I asked her at once.

"Should I? Let bygones be bygones. That's my philosophy."

"How can you talk like that! Wasn't it you who hurt him badly? Now he won't be able to attend class for at least two weeks, the doctor says!" I was a bit beside myself.

"Who cares? Why did he get in my way?" She was mad at me, to my surprise. "You Chinese people have a tendency of getting into other people's way. That's just the trouble with you guys," she added.

Her unreasonable argument made me lose my temper. Trembling violently, I cursed her as well as I could. People in the hall raised heads from their bowls to look at us. Marie didn't expect this from me; when she had controlled herself, she rushed out.

After that we seldom, if ever, spoke to each other.

Johnson told me Marie had bought her skates in Austria, from where her parents immigrated to Canada. Therefore, the skates must have meant a great deal to her.

Having heard my description of the dining hall incident, Johnson said jokingly that one of Marie's forefathers might have been a soldier in the Eight-Power Allied Forces in 1900, fighting the Boxers. This might account for her prejudice against the Chinese.

I didn't believe the story, but I didn't doubt that she was a racist. "Suppose. she had hurt one of her own countrymen," I said, "would she have acted in such a rude, cold-blooded way? And the hypocrite keeps telling us how she loves us."

"Well, honestly, I don't think she particularly intended to look down upon you people," Johnson tried to soothe me. "Racial discrimination is out of the question here. She is nuts, rude, and selfish, too. Maybe she hasn't lied. Maybe she does love your people and all the people in the world. Yet her love is in an abstract sense, in a spiritual sense. You know Ralph Wald Emerson, the American philosopher? He said 'I love man, but not men.' So does Marie. So do lots of Westerners."

Dear reader, what do you think of my friend Johnson's idea?

A Purse

He Ai

THERE are people you meet every day, yet when you are asked to say something about them, you don't know what to say. There are other people you see only once in your lifetime, yet you will never forget them. The following is a story about an American I met only once for a short time, yet I know I'll remember her all my life.

She was at the head of the line, waiting to get on the Greyhound bus at San Francisco, and I was just behind her. I liked to get a seat in the front of the bus so that I would be able to have a good view of the scene on the way. She was a heavily built woman not much taller than me, wearing a purple and blue skirt and blouse. She was carrying a bag in her right hand and a big basket in her left. Our conversation started naturally when I offered to carry the bag for her.

"Oh, thank you. That's real kind of you. The bag *is* too much for me."

She let me carry the bag for her when we were getting on the bus. I took the seat by the window in the front row, right behind the driver; she took the seat on my right. I put her bag on the rail above and she put her big basket under her seat.

When everything was settled, she smiled at me, and said, "Thanks a lot." I looked at her and noticed that she had a remarkably round face. Her eyes were large and very expressive, and the dimples on her face gave her smile a special charm. Her hair was curly and grey, like a circle of white embroidery around her black face. If not for the contrast, I wouldn't have noticed her race. Her dimpled smile told me she was a very kind woman. I was happy to have a seat beside this kind, maternal person.

She pointed at the basket under her seat and said: "Want to have some cheese?"

I shook my head and told her: "No, thanks. We Chinese are not used to having cheese."

"Oh, but this is good cheese! Homemade cheese. I made it myself for my grandson.... But did you say you Chinese don't eat cheese? What about cookies? I've made some cookies too, sugar cookies, ginger cookies.... You want some?"

This time I knew I could not say no. It was just not right to reject the kind offer of a mother. She took some cookies from her basket. They were delicious. I had had cookies of many kinds at the homes of my friends, but I must say hers were the best.

"You do make very good cookies," I said.

"Oh, thank you. Have more," she said.

"You are from China? Do you Chinese make cookies, too?" I told her we did, but not exactly the same kinds.

Then she began to tell me about her family.

95

"You know, I'm going to Los Angeles to see my son and my daughter-in-law; they are teaching at a university there," she told me proudly.

"You must be proud of them," I said.

"Oh, yeah! We, both of us, me and my old man, thought it important to give him a good education. We did our best and he didn't let us down...."

"But you know," she continued, "this time I am going there for my grandson. Oh, you don't know what a nice boy he is! He's going to be three. He's a big boy now. Didn't I tell you it's his birthday tomorrow? I've made the cheese, the cookies and a big cake all for him."

What a loving grandma! Her words were as fragrant as the smell coming from her big basket. The wrinkles on her face were ironed out by her smile. What a charming face!

"You are from China? Oh, how nice! But it's very far from here....

"You are here all by yourself leaving your child at home? Oh, you must be homesick....

"You are going home soon? Oh, you must be happy! You'll soon see your dear boy again....

"You are going to Los Angeles, too? Have you ever been there....

"Your first trip there? Oh, you must be careful."

She looked at my handbag and asked:

"You put your passport and money there?"

I told her I did.

"Oh, daughter, you must never be so careless. You don't know Los Angeles. It won't do to have your money and passport in your handbag. Oh, it won't do! If you lose them, you'll be in trouble, in real trouble!"

I had heard about Los Angeles and I knew I had to be careful. But I couldn't think of another way to keep my money and passport, so I didn't say anything but smiled. She must have read my mind because the next moment she put her hands on her chest and said:

"You see, I have a little hand-sewn bag hanging here. That is the way I keep my money when I travel."

While saying this, she took a purse out from under her blue and purple blouse. It was an oblong shape made of a brown material. She grinned at me and put it back.

"You know this is a wonderful place to keep your purse. You know what, if anyone dares touch this part of you, daughter, you just yell. Nobody dares do that to you. It is a safe place."

I told her I thought it was a good idea.

We went on chatting. When she learned that I was going to visit the Grand Canyon, she advised me to buy some heavy clothes:

"The shirt and pants you are wearing are far from enough. It can be very cold out there though it is still warm here. You'll freeze to death, daughter, if you go there in these clothes." I thanked her for her kind advice.

"You can get some clothes real cheap. You don't need to buy those fancy things. Just a heavy coat will do." Then she began to tell me how to find places in Los Angeles to get the clothes, which bus to take, and where to get an extension.

We dozed off sometimes, but when we woke up, we went on with our conversation. We ate cookies and later a little cheese, too, and that was how I began to take a liking for cheese. To be with her was never boring; on the contrary, it was a real pleasure. All the way I seldom looked out the window, even though I had the best possible seat for a view. I never regretted it. After all, how often could I have a chance to be so close to a kind American mother like her, and how many Chinese have had an experience like this?

By the time we got close to Los Angeles, it was getting dark. She smiled and her face glowed when she said: "Oh, I'll soon be with my dear, dear grandson."

I was happy for her and told her so. Then she took my hands in hers.

"Daughter, you must promise me one thing. You must promise me that you are going to sew a little purse like mine as soon as you get to Los Angeles."

I looked at her and was touched by her concern. I smiled but didn't answer her at first. How could I promise to sew a purse if I had neither cloth, nor needle, nor thread?

"Daughter, you've got to promise me!"

I knew she was worrying for me, afraid that I would get into trouble if I lost my passport and money. I felt the warmth of her hands holding mine and promised that I would sew it. I knew I was lying but I did not want to disappoint her.

I've never met her again. I didn't even ask her

name. To me she was just a mother and a grand-mother. The memory of the warmth of her hands and the recollection of the beauty of her heart will remain in my mind forever.

Call the Police: *A Tale*

Lydia He Liu

W HEN in Rome, do as the Romans do. With
a slight change, the universal proverbial wisdom
would go: "When in Rome, hear as the Romans do."
Indeed, travelling from Shanghai to Boston means
switching from one source of noise to another.
There is nothing you can do but get your ears
attuned as soon as you arrive.

Having been brought up with a variety of local
noises: shouts across the street, truck horns, factory
whistles, quarrelling neighbours, fights on the public bus, good-hearted warnings shouted regularly
through a loud-speaker in the department store that
made you look furtively around in the manner
more of a thief than a potential victim, I found
myself suddenly transposed into a world of silence
by a round-the-clock flight from Shanghai to Boston.

People whispered in the coffee shop, at the street
corner, in the office and at home. Cars, vans, trucks,
all seemed to whisper around good-manneredly,
with two notable exceptions — the police cars and
fire engines. These two species ran at top speed,
sirens blaring at top volume so that they looked

pompous and efficient. They certainly (*Even at this very moment I hear a police car fast approaching and judging from the sound it must be about two blocks away*) kept the city in good order.

Surely there could never be a more law-abiding people than the residents of Boston. So much depends on the cops, (*No, I was wrong. Two police cars, instead of one, are now racing by right under my window, sirens going like mad*) without whom life would stand still.

The week after my arrival, Julie, a friend, took me to her favourite Chinese restaurant for dinner.

While waiting for our order, I looked around, sipped my tea, and chatted with my friend. The interior was decorated in a loudly traditional Chinese style, more traditional than anything I had ever seen in China (*A police siren emerges somewhere; as it closes in, it becomes more and more shrill; it is passing under my window and now it's gone*) — crimson tables, crimson napkins, crimson light shades — crimson all over the place. I was beginning to feel heated up despite the air-conditioned hall when a bright object swam into my view. It was a man's broad forehead with a slightly bald top, the possessor of which came to a halt at the table opposite ours and seated himself in a dignified manner. In the fragment of a minute, he was again on his feet, unbuttoning his expensive-looking grey suit, which he folded up fondly and placed on the next seat. He then resumed the seat. Every now and then his eyes would bend down and examine the impeccable pink shirt and the smart-looking vest that he had on. He was one of the most self-confident men I had ever seen.

The food was wonderful but not quite authentic. Julie said that most Americans preferred it this way.

A clear peal of laughter put a momentary stop to the humming, murmuring, and whispering sound that had been going on around me ever since I came in. It came from the table next to the well-groomed man. A young student and his girlfriend were hugging and laughing. They were in high spirits and seemed to be celebrating some special occasion, for the young man was holding a champagne bottle in his left hand. Their respectable-looking neighbour, being disturbed, peered over his shoulder at the boisterous couple for a moment and turned back to the paper he had been reading. I noticed it was the business page of the *Boston Globe*.

Pop... splash... something must have gone wrong, for our business man jumped up all of a sudden and glared at the young couple. His head was streaming with white foaming liquid, which trickled down along his ears, along his starched white collar and was fast encroaching upon his elegant vest. He cursed and wiped himself with a napkin. The young man was helping, apologizing, looking foolish. He was terribly sorry that he had been clumsy with the bottle but the pressure had been unusually strong and that the cork somehow popped out. He said he felt so bad that he'd rather stay away from champagne for the rest of his life than ruin the gentleman's clothes. The businessman fixed the young student with angry eyes as if he would like to wring his neck. But he did nothing of the sort, merely pointing out that the other had no business sitting back to back with him. The accident hushed the festive spirit of the couple. For a space of ten minutes they were very quiet, wearing a guilty look. The businessman picked up his paper, put it down, examined his vest which had some wet spots and his shirt which was in a frightful state. He fumed. (*Again the screech of a police car breaks in and interrupts everything. It's gone. Thank God.*) He turned around, staring in anger at the young man and the young woman for a few seconds, and went back to his paper. Again he threw it down, examined the wet fingers, fuming and flushing. He picked up the paper again, seemed to be absorbed in it for a little while, but grew impatient, and threw it away, his hand beginning to drum on the table.

He stood up.

The young couple looked anxious. He walked past them and stalked firmly across the hall. He came straight to the cashier and showed her the state of his clothes. The cashier sympathized and apologized that it had happened in her restaurant but that he need not be upset because the restaurant would gladly clean them for him as compensation.

— "But I want to call the police."

— "Well..."

— "I must call the police. Could I use your phone?"

— "But really there is no need to disturb the cops over this. Let's see.... Are you sure that the cops can help nearly as much as we? I said we are going to clean it for you at our own expense. How about that?"

—"They will not get away with it! No. They must pay for it!"

....

—"Your order, Sir." The waiter showed up with his food.

—"All right, we'll talk about it after dinner."

His anger subsided visibly at the sight of the food. He turned on his heels and was back at his table in a second. While his jaws moved up and down busily, the tense muscles around his eyes seemed to relax.

I asked my friend what the cops would do if he had called them.

—"Nothing, I suppose."

She began telling me her own experience with the police when she went to the graduate school at Boston University.

It was three years ago. She had just moved into a semi-basement apartment with a single window opening towards the street. There was a tiny patch of lawn under the window which she seldom opened but, when she did, a strange, offensive odour would come in. She was puzzled by the odour for a while but soon found out the cause. Every once in a while, a group of teenagers would gather at night on the lawn, singing, fooling around and getting drunk. Then they would urinate underneath her window. As soon as she discovered this, she reported it to the police. Two policemen came, asked questions, and took notes. There were forms to be filled out as usual. Her name? ... Male or female? ... Marital status? She said that the last piece of information was not likely to help them in their investigation but they went through the forms. Three weeks later she had to call in the police again because she still couldn't open the window without letting in the stench. They arrived, questioned, took notes. There were more forms to be filled out. Name? ... Male or female? ... Marital status? ... In the end, one of the policemen suggested that she buy a water pistol, put her own urine in it and shoot at the kids if they did it again. A month passed and nothing happened. She continued to suffer from the stench. So she called again and the policemen came. Name? ... Male or female? ... Marital status? ... Upon leaving, one of the policemen made a suggestion that she fix a power cord outside the window and electrify the trouble-makers if she wanted. In the end, she had to leave the apartment and the police.

By the time our businessman finished his dinner, he had regained his former composure, confidence, and dignity. He settled the account with the cashier and was about to leave when the cashier reminded him of his clothes.

—"Oh, that's OK. I'll fix it myself."

The young couple breathed a great sigh of relief and came back to life.

(*Deafening screech. I can't go on with my story. What is it? Three police cars have pulled up under my window. A funny turn of events. Speak of the devil and he's sure to come. Have they appeared because I am writing about them? Let's see.*) They are speaking to

Marie-Anne, the ex-girlfriend of my downstairs neighbour Richard. Richard has been complaining lately that Marie-Anne prowls outside his apartment every night and tries to disturb his sleep because he has a new date called Lisa. He was furious and threatened that if she went on like this he would certainly call the police. So he did.

Name?

....

Gender?

....

Marital status?

....

The Melting Pot and the Mosaic: A Comparison of Americans and Canadians

Chen Zhongming, Wang Xiao'ou, and Chang Yuemin

"How can you tell an American from a Canadian?" This is the problem that has puzzled us as Chinese ever since as we set foot on North American soil. Well, it racks American and Canadian brains, too. If you pose such a question, either in Times Square in New York or at the Bay (a department store) in Toronto, nine out of ten times they would be hard put to come up with an answer.

And the answers, predictably, vary a great deal from one person to another. In fact, they are so many and varied — regarding virtually everything — that we can hardly enumerate them here. However, some patterns do emerge that allow us to distinguish the people of the two nations. Moreover, in the past few years we have tested some of the answers to see if they really apply. Though it is difficult to make a clear-cut distinction, it is our hope that one day you can try these methods to tell the difference between an American and a Canadian.

First of all, we deem it necessary to draw your attention to the metaphors the North Americans are fond of. When you ask either a Canadian or an American to give you a general idea of the U.S. and Canada in a word or two, he or she would, more often than not, refer to the United States as the Melting Pot. To put it simply, it is a place where everything melts and reshapes itself. But the allusion to Canada is the Mosaic. An artifact immediately comes to mind: it is produced by joining together small pieces of glass or stone of different colours. An observant eye will see that different elements in a mosaic, although they combine to form a single picture, remain distinct elements. In a word, they do not really mix or change a great deal. Yet however graphic or vivid the Melting Pot and Mosaic metaphors are, such generalized comparisons appear superficial and facile without some examples.

If you are sufficiently curious, we believe that further questions would reveal the nature of these two vivid metaphors. The United States, our American friends tell us, is like a melting pot that "melts," as it were, people's different features and reproduces something new. We may gather that this means that people from different nations of the world mix with one another to become a single nationality. American cosmopolitan cities — New York, Boston, Detroit, Chicago, Los Angeles, San Francisco — are but a few such examples. In lifestyle, immigrants are not supposed to stick too much to their own customs or rituals, either tribal, racial, or national. "Do in Rome as the Romans do" is as good an axiom as any we can offer you. And it is little wonder that we see people of different colours — white, yellow, black, brown and so on — everywhere we go. In terms of clothes, food, lodging, and transportation, you may see the Chinese eating Italian pizza, or Englishmen eating sushi, Filipinos living in Gothic-styled houses, or a Japanese driving an American-made car with a French girlfriend. There are no limits to people's likes or dislikes, it would seem: people just follow the general trend.

Canada, on the other hand, is quite different from the Melting Pot, though, at first sight, it may look deceptively like the U.S. in some respects. For instance, regarding national make-up, a Canadian professor from Ottawa once claimed that Canada matched or even outstripped the U.S. in taking in immigrants from all parts of the world. Also, Canadians enjoy as much freedom as their neighbours to the south, both in lifestyle and many other things. But the overall similarities would end just about here. We do notice some differences in these somewhat similar qualities. For one thing, Canadians stress diversity and tolerance in their life rather than conformity (in the sense of melting the old to re-form a homogeneous whole), or even uniformity. Indeed, in America the pressure of conformity is sometimes so oppressive that many literary works attack its evils and appeal to the American public to eliminate them. J.D. Salinger wrote *The Catcher in the Rye*, showing the agony of an adolescent entering the conformist adult world. Joseph Heller's *Catch-22* further illustrated the conformity and regimentation in the army that drove young American soldiers half crazy and reduced them to unthinking beings. Similarly, Ken Kesey's *One Flew Over the Cuckoo's Nest* continued the theme by depicting the ever-increasing conformity in American society, a conformity enforced by putting nonconformists in jails or mental hospitals. There is racial prejudice, especially when people from other nations do not readily conform to the prevalent American way of life. In sharp contrast, there are not so many works dealing with conformity by Canadian writers.

There is no strict government control over people's lifestyle in Canada. Canadian multiculturalism, quite unique and successful in the present world context, contributes greatly to the Canadian character. Multiculturalism is encouraged by the government and favoured and practised by the people; it prevents different racial or national traits or habits from disappearing; it advocates the enhancement rather than the submerging of divergent national or racial characteristics. In a word, peaceful coexistence and harmony prevail over the "melting" and "reshaping" so often seen in the States.

People originally from different nations live together peacefully in Canada. The native Indians have their own reserves and cling to their way of life. Other minority groups like the Ukrainians, the Italians, the Japanese, the Chinese, and so on also keep their own cultural and religious traditions. The

Americans, on the other hand, have an infamous history of hunting the Indians like animals. *The Last of the Mohicans* by American writer, James Fenimore Cooper, is but one early literary indictment of such an inhuman act. *Uncle Tom's Cabin* revealed the shameful treatment of blacks by whites. Mistreatment of blacks moved an American black leader, Martin Luther King, to campaign for civil rights for blacks. More recently, an American movie, *The Atlanta Child Murders*, was a fictionalized account of racial prejudice against blacks in the late seventies. All of these reflect the social milieu of the American society.

In sharp contrast, *A Dream Like Mine* by Canadian writer M.T. Kelly, about Canadian natives' cherished dream, won the 1987 Governor-General's Literary Award. This is not to eulogize the Canadians and defame the Americans. Although there are instances of Canadian ill-treatment of Indians and of the Chinese in the past, or of the Japanese during World War II, racial distinctions and prejudice are less overt in Canada than in America. Further, a very recent compensation (September 1988) made by the Canadian government to the Japanese shows the Canadian effort to achieve fairness and racial harmony.

What is more, in Canada, different nationalities often hold annual celebrations together to keep alive their respective cuisines, costumes, dances, music, and culture. We were deeply impressed by such gatherings when we were in Ottawa, Canada's capital, and Calgary, host city of the 1988 Winter Olympic Games. If you are a gourmet, you can spend little or no money in relishing much delicious food. Likewise, people interested in costumes, dancing, and so on, can learn much from these galas of many nationalities. All of this is an example of the Canadian spirit of coexistence and tolerance.

Another factor — bilingualism — also adds, in more ways than one, to this harmonious and peaceful relationship between the Canadian people. Whereas the States has one official language, Canada boasts a bilingual tradition as long as its history. Both French and English are official languages and spoken across the country. Despite many disturbances over the French-English language issue, especially in Quebec in the sixties, the Canadians have learned to treat both languages and cultures with equal respect. Just as multiculturalism has preserved the legends, traditions, and customs of many other nationalities, so bilingualism has preserved the two major languages and cultures. Further, according to Wilder Penfield's arguments in "The Superiority of the Bilingual Brain," (*Modern Canadian Essays*) the bilingual environment helps develop the intellectual faculty. More importantly, it further cultivates Canadians' tolerant and open attitude.

Closely related to this national atmosphere of coexistence and mutual respect are personal traits. Whereas multiculturalism and bilingualism foster the Canadians' tolerant and temperate nature, Americans, lacking such societal circumstances, are in general less patient and less tolerant in their attitude towards racial and ethnic differences. Though we have seen Americans marvelling curiously at the bilingual labels or instructions on some Canadian products, we have also heard Americans speaking impatiently about Canada's having two official languages as unnecessary.

So, if you want to distinguish an American from a Canadian, not by posing the blunt question "Are you an American?" or "Where are you from?" but in a tactical way, you may want to probe their attitudes towards multiculturalism and bilingualism. Canadians would be positive about these two concepts, whereas most Americans tend to favour a one-culture and one-language social environment, that is, the result of the melting-pot effect. A further hint: some Americans may not even know these two terms, whereas most Canadians understand them at the slightest mention.

Americans are also different from Canadians on the individual level. First of all, Americans have the reputation of being open and straight forward. Whether they are glad or angry, they tell you how they feel and what they think directly and openly. To us Chinese, Americans seem to verbalize virtually everything, including such sensitive matters as sexuality or marital affairs. We once had a class in which some American women engaged in a talk about their own sexuality, which embarrassed us. The Canadians, by contrast, tend to be more circumspect about sex or similar issues. Also, though Canadians are less inhibited than the Chinese regarding social taboos, they do not go as far as Americans in expressing their feelings bluntly. Their sentiments are more controlled, and they will make a point of smoothing over difficult issues when they occur. Canadians are closer to the Chinese in this respect than the Americans.

Second, compared with Canadians, Americans are less formal in social gatherings and more lively in temperament. While Americans would wear a bizarre hair-style and flashy clothes and dance wildly at a party, Canadians are normally well-groomed, well-dressed and dance gently. You can detect the British gentleman-like quality in Canadian behaviour. In 1966, Frank Watt asked this question: "Should they (Canadians) be calm, urbane and ironical in the tradition of upper-class England, or should they be cheerful, lively and brash like the true North Americans; healthy peasants, or angry young men? Is their country 'American attic, an empty room,' or 'the big land' with 'the big ale'?" (*Nationalism in Canada*) We hold that Canadians, even after twenty years or so since the question was posed, still keep alive much of the English sense of propriety. We may use one example to show this point. Before we landed in North America, we had learned that the rejoinders to "Thank you," or "Thank you very much (ever so much)" are "Not at all," "Don't metion it," or "You're welcome." During our two-year stay in the U.S., we never heard people reply with "Not at all." In Canada, we got one "not at all" when we thanked a professor. In most cases, Canadians would reply by saying "(You're) welcome" or "(It's) my pleasure" or "With pleasure." Americans, we have noticed, like to use such short and terse phrases as "Anytime," "Sure," and "No problem," though Canadians sometimes also use them. A touch of casualness and disinterestedness is easily detectable in the American expressions. Indeed, some Americans do not even say "thank you" when it is considered to be required. An American tourist guide from San Francisco says about Canadians: "They're very polite.... And they always say thank you."

Thirdly, Americans enjoy their materialism, although not necessarily "selfish individualism," a term Chinese are fond of using to denote its negative aspect. Canadians, unlike Americans, cherish spiritual life and the sense of community and togetherness. Although "the Promised Land" refers to North America as a whole, nowadays people tend to mean only the U.S. when they use it. For Americans it holds forth the prospect of opportunity, equality, and democracy. We can safely say that America was and still is a land in which many people want to make their dreams come true, dreams which are sometimes generalized as "the American Dream." This American Dream has inspired famous American statesmen like Benjamin Franklin in the 18th century, and businessmen like Lee Iacocca in this century. Canadians are less likely to make their fortunes as quickly as the Americans. We have heard Canadians saying: "If you want to make fast money, go to the States."

But behind this veneer of the rich and prosperous American life, people with insight question the single-mindedness of material pursuit. Take Henry

David Thoreau, a great nineteenth century American thinker, for example. In his book *Walden* he compared the advantages and disadvantages of American life. His thinking was apparently triggered by rampant materialism and disregard for the spiritual life. He chose what he called "voluntary poverty" in order to better view the nature of American materialism. Canadians, it would seem, are less obsessed with this aspect of the American Dream. F.P. Grove, a famous Canadian writer, deplored the corrupted American ideal in his *A Search for America*. Another important Canadian nationalist writer, Hugh MacLennan, has also on several occasions attacked the self-seeking and materialism of the American business community. On the whole, Canadians just take life as it comes. They are not so obsessed about being a millionaire. They are quite content with their life. On a per capita-basis, more Canadians than Americans devote their time to studying the *Bible* or going to church. These religious Canadians (and those Americans who are sincere religious people) emphasize the quality of life, rather than the amount of money they can make.

Tightly connected to this attitude is the rhythm of life in the U.S. and Canada. The American tempo is quicker, even to the point of hurry or hastiness, while Canadians take their time and do things at their own pace. Because some Americans are busy with making a living through tough competition, with making a lot of money, or with enjoying life, they are less likely to take note of your needs. In big cities like New York or Los Angeles, you see people just passing by without doing so much as casting a glance at you. Their behaviour sometimes leaves the impression that Americans are not friendly or hospitable. But you may want to make some allowance for that, since you now know at least part of the reason why they are always in a hurry, on the move. Our visits between the States and Canada have given us many chances to observe this phenomenon. One example here will suffice to tell the difference. At the Greyhound bus terminal in Niagara Falls we saw two line-ups: one going to other Canadian cities, the other going to the States. Those going to the States, mostly Americans, were standing alone, attending to their own business, while the Canadian queue was alive with conversation. It also happens that Canadians seem much more friendly, in the sense that they greet you or smile at you. They may readily help you when you are in trouble.

On the other hand, Americans are more alert, independent, efficient, and competitive, perhaps a result of having to keep up the rivalry with others. By comparison, Canadians lead an easy and sometimes "dull" life. We put "dull" in quotation marks because one of our Canadian friends said it. Canadians may even seem a bit lazy to our Chinese way of thinking, since they do not have to work as hard as we do to make a decent living. This fact owes much to their relatively small population living in a vast land (the second largest in the world) with many natural resources to export. With the help of modern facilities and technology mainly from the

States, Canadians do not need to exert themselves as much as Americans, but still share more or less the same standard of living as the latter.

Fourthly, most Americans are, by comparison with Canadians, prouder, more out-going, pushy and even aggressive. They think of America as the No. 1 country in the world. This undue pride occasionally expresses itself in personal relationships in the form of aggression or interference. In a way, Americans want their own lives left alone, but they want to take charge of your life. Canadians, on the other hand, would not be so meddling, overbearing or domineering. Suppose you were asked to play basketball by an American or a Canadian and are reluctant to do so. The American would "buddy" you into playing while the Canadian would leave you in peace. Though it is true there may be Americans who are not like that, it is also true that many of them match our description.

In terms of political and international life, Americans are both more radical and interventionist, whereas Canada is more temperate and keeps its nose within Canadian territory. Americans hate the word and the concept of "Communism" as much as, if not more than, we Chinese hate prostitutes in our society. The States, being the strongest bastion of the Western capitalist world, has never ceased to resist all Communist or Socialist influences. Further, the American military presence in many parts of the world (i.e. Korea, Taiwan, the Middle East, etc.) is too blatant and aggressive to be justified by any excuse.

Canada does not go to that extreme. Politically, it has adopted such socialist elements as welfare payments, unemployment insurance, public education, health insurance and so on. The image of Canadians in the eyes of the international community is also more favourable: it is one of peace-loving and peace-keeping. Americans, on the contrary, generally present themselves as international police. Here, it is quite clear that the national policy of the U.S. and of Canada have subtly affected the personalities of their respective peoples. Thus, one way to judge whether someone is an American or a Canadian is very simple: just ask for his opinions about the role he would like his country to play in the international political arena. You will be surprised to see how often the differences between a Canadian and an American show up.

There is still another point of comparison, which exists in relationships between men and women. Canadians, especially men, differ from their American counterparts in their attitude towards the fair sex. American males at present are somewhat like the Chinese, in the sense that they share housework with their wives, women are employed in important positions and paid equal money for the same jobs as men do. In quite a number of ways, American women are in fact competing successfully with American males. A conservative critic has even written an article entitiled "The Loss of Masculinity of the American Male," lamenting the many changes, or rather interchanges, of male-female roles in social, economic, and political life.

It is worth mentioning that the drastic transformation in male-female relationships has a lot to do with the feminist movement, which started in the sixties and spread like fire across the States. Though some people have blamed this movement for the present promiscuous sexuality (often in the form of premarital and extramarital sex) and AIDS in America, a fundamental change has taken place in almost every aspect of life involving male-female relationships. The whole concept of women as men's equals in the full sense of the word, not merely as sex objects, has taken root in America. In the American market or at the universities, you can see many books on such matters as: the different roles women can play in stabilizing and moderating family and social relations (feminist sociology); women's unique sensibilities and ways of perceiving and writing (gender study); different language and imagery used by women in writing and speech (discourse analysis); the possibility of dismantling the present male-dominated American society and of re-writing the Bible and history in light of feminist concepts (feminist-deconstructionist theory), and so on.

Canadian male-female relationships, by contrast, seem to be blemished by inequality and by lack of change. We heard an American TV production assistant commenting on this: "The Canadian male is a chauvinist pig, about 10 years behind here." (You see, the American is quite frank and even a bit harsh. It proves our point mentioned above.) It is only very recently that Canadians picked up the

120

above-mentioned topics and set out to change the undesirable aspects of Canadian relations between the sexes. Many Canadian men do not take women as seriously as they do their fellow men, paying mostly lip-service to the feminist movement or to women's grievances. This fact may partially account for Canada's divorce rate, the highest in the world in 1985 (about 51%). However, we hasten to add that the traditional sense of family still prevails in Canada, whereas in the States this concept has been shattered. There are millions of single parent families and many more bachelors and spinsters in the U.S.

A sure way to tell an American apart from a Canadian is to ask his or her opinion about the feminist movement, or any issue related to male-female relationships. Americans would be more ready to talk and more likely to support a larger role for women; Canadians, in most cases, seem to be reticent about this, and would stick to traditional, male-centred values.

The geography and landmarks of Canada and the United States also say something about the two peoples. Canada and the U.S. share the Rockies and the Niagara Falls — the longest mountain range and the greatest waterfall in the world — and the five Great Lakes (Lake Superior, Lake Michigan, Lake Huron, Lake Erie, and Lake Ontario). Further, they claim to have the longest undefended border in the world, a sign of peace between the two countries. Both Americans and Canadians are proud of this. There are, of course, unique features to each country. The Yellowstone National Park, the Grand Canyon, and the Statue of Liberty would be among the first to be mentioned if you asked an American about points of tourist interest.

A Canadian would talk about Banff National Park, the CN Tower in Toronto — the world's highest free-standing man-made structure — the Thousand Islands and Quebec city, where you can relive history. Or he would mention the Trans-Canada Highway — the longest highway in the world, the West Edmonton Mall — the world's largest roofed mall, the Olympic Oval in Calary — the largest covered skating rink in the world or the aurora borealis (Northern Lights). If you are not certain whether you are facing an American or a Canadian, just try asking him or her for information on these scenic spots or areas of interest.

We have discussed many salient American and Canadian characteristics. If one of our methods or categories happen to be ineffective, please try again; or try the next one. And remember, there are always exceptions to the rules.

A Nightmarish Scene from Life

Shujuan Li

ONE evening I went to a movie called *The Rocky Horror Picture Show* at the Physical Science Auditorium on campus. As usual, I took out $3.75 and handed it to a man in his forties who sold the tickets at the door. He cast a glance at me and asked, "Are you Japanese?" "No, I'm not," I replied. He uttered a little sound and nodded his head. Then he put a ticket in my hand and warned me in a very low tone, "Please take a back seat."

I felt he was acting a little odd. Don't people usually choose their own seats? Why did he tell me to take a back seat? Although I didn't understand, I did what he said and sat down in a back seat.

The Auditorium was dim and smoky and filled with odd-looking young people. Some had dyed their hair different colours: red, blue, yellow, green and black; some had painted their faces in various ways; some wore all black suits; some men were dressed up like women with heavy makeup. Whistles and shouts could be heard at times.

Soon I felt that something was strange and a few

minutes later I felt I was in danger. Rice was flung into the back rows from the front of the Auditorium. The people in the back seats began to fight back with squirt guns and bottles. I huddled to avoid this unexpected attack, but at the same time I was quite pleased that I was not sitting in the middle seats, in which case I would have taken the brunt of it all. I hoped the film would start soon so that all this would come to an end.

But things got even worse after the lights went off. Some crazy Rocky fans danced in front of the screen, touched it, shouted and sang songs along with the actors in the film. As the ruby lips in the film's opening credits give way to a wedding attended by normal-looking conservative young Americans, Brad Majors and Janet Weiss, rice started flying in the air again. When the two young lovers in the film got stranded in the rain, people in the front rows and back rows doused each other with their water guns. I dodged about trying not to get wet.

"You can use this to protect yourself," a man beside me said while handing over his straw hat. He was suffering, too.

"What nasty people!" I cursed them silently and wanted to leave the noisy and dirty place immediately. But my curiosity about the film and the audience's behaviour made me stay.

The film continued. When Brad and Janet saw "a light over at the Frankenstein's place," dozens of lighters, flashlights and matches illuminated the Auditorium. It was the first time in my life that I had to suffer to see a movie.

The film finally ended. My head was aching. I returned the hat to the man beside me and walked out of the Auditorium with him. He told me that these Rocky fans came to see the film each time it was shown so they had memorized the dialogue and the songs in the film. He said he knew a person who had seen it 873 times. And each time they would throw rice and shoot water guns and leave a great mess behind them when the film was over.

A few days later I came across a review in a magazine which helped me better understand what happened that night at the Auditorium.

The Rocky Horror Picture Show is an outcome of the countercultural movement. When the film was released in 1975, it was not very popular. But ten years later, this rock-'n'-roll travesty had earned over $60 million at midnight movie houses.

The Rocky Horror Picture Show is more than a sleeper hit for insomniacs. It is a cross-generational phenomenon, an evocation of '50s monster movies wrapped in the anything-goes spirit of the '60s that found a niche in the '70s and has blossomed in the '80s into a rite of passage for millions of American teenagers. As Richard O'Brien, the 43-year-old New Zealand-born Londoner who wrote Rocky's script, music and lyrics, noted on its tenth anniversary, "The movie is really an excuse for dressing up and having a party."

Only then did I completely awake from my nightmare.

The movie was a shock to me, but the scene in the Auditorium affected me even more. I think these were young Americans representing a part of the new generation. Their actions were just as ridiculous as the movie. It was the first shock, perhaps a cultural shock, I got after I arrived in America.

Unlike traditional Chinese who are usually brought up with strict discipline and taught to be quiet, tolerant and practise self-restraint in their early years, young Americans grow up more independently and freely. They are frank, energetic, easily excited and influenced by others and feel free to express their feelings.

A bizarre movie like *The Rocky Horror Picture Show* can only be spawned by a society that is tolerant of all types of people and ideas, and which is willing to tolerate the discomforts they may sometimes bring.

Behind the Black Suit, White Shirt and Red Tie

Wu Ping

IF you hear that somebody is a lawyer in America, you can safely assume that he is one of those middle, or upper middle class people who live a relatively easy life. Every day, Morris Kalish goes to his office in a law firm in his black suit and white shirt with a red tie, the dress code for the millions of lawyers who penetrate every phase of American society. Every day, he is either answering inquiries over the phone, having a hearing in court, or writing briefs which are, in his own words, "boring enough so that the reader is half asleep by the time he gets to the point." What we are interested in here is something behind that dress code: how does he, like millions of others, live as a husband, a parent, a friend and an individual in society? Snap shots from these phases of his life help to povide answers to the question that my Chinese friends ask me so often: How do Americans live?

Contrary to the traditional Chinese concept, the base for an American family is "two" individuals and not "one" family. Some people may think that this is the same. Far from it. The obvious difference between "one" and "two" makes all the difference. Morris has his own bank accounts and credit cards. He was greatly surprised to learn that my wife could look at my bills. It is his own business, and his freedom as a husband as well, how he spends his money. Of course, there are joint responsibilities. But even here it is clearly laid out and strictly followed. The husband is responsible for the lion's share of the family expenditure, like the payment for the house and the utility bills, the groceries and the education of the children. The wife takes care of her own clothing (buying clothing is a big business in America, you not only buy what you need, as is the case for many Chinese, you buy what you want) and pays the baby-sitter. Although the responsibilities vary from family to family, the idea of "bread winner" and the "house wife" is fading, especially among double income families like Morris and his wife.

Five busy days in a week with dinner time for "information exchange" once a day seems to leave no room for affection between the couple. As a matter of fact, each seems to be so busy with his or her duties during weekdays that pent-up emotions are left for the weekend. That's why the Saturday night "out" is so important for them. But even on the weekend, joint breakfast is not common, unless there are activities after breakfast. To be able to sleep as late as he wants is a personal freedom Morris has only twice a week and he is not ready to give that up. Starting from Monday, he looks forward to Saturday, a time when he doesn't have to get up early and have a shower and shave and appear smart in his suit and tie. It is so good to be able to wear your "play clothes," as his four-year-old daughter Dana puts it, and sit with your feet on the table. So good to behave the way you want and not the way you have to. How tragic it would be if the husband and the wife did most things together, as is still cherished by many Chinese. If his wife wants to go shopping, she never tries to drag him along.

Saturday evening is a different story. Here being together is always appealing to Morris. It is the time when he can sit with his wife and have a nice conversation without the presence of the kids. Going to a movie after dinner at a restaurant is the "norm" for passing the night. The kids, of course, are again in the care of a temporary baby-sitter. It's hard for many Chinese to imagine that parents would go to a restaurant, where they spend approximately the same amount of money on one meal as they do for the rest of the week's food, as well as paying between $15 to $20 to a baby-sitter who only knows how to dial 911 in case of emergency. They also have the trouble of taking the baby-sitter home in the middle of the night. Morris thinks differently. The money for the meal, the movie tickets and the fee for the baby-sitter is actually nothing compared with the freedom and the time of being together. This is the only time during which many Americans can recreate their "honeymoon" and show affection to each other. Otherwise they have to wait for such once-a-year occasions as their wedding anniversary and birthdays.

For Morris, a good weekend consists of the following: no responsibilities assigned by the wife to take care of the kids, no obligation to catch up in the office, a good movie and dinner at a nice restaurant and pleasant weather. Such a good weekend would become perfect and memorable if the dinner is of spare ribs and the Boston Red Sox baseball team wins.

Three times in a year, affection for each other gets to the surface of life in the form of a "surprise." Unfortunately, it is getting more and more difficult to have a "surprise" now. Knowing what they have in mind, I said to him "a surprise for Anita?" when I saw him come home one day with a birthday cake for his wife's 42nd birthday. "She is not very smart if it is still a surprise after these many years!" he replied. In a society where material need is not urgent, the best gift is more spiritual than material, similar to "buying a smile for the loved" that Jia Baoyu (hero of *A Dream of Red Mansions*) tried so hard to do. To make arrangements so that Anita could meet her best friend on her birthday at a fancy hotel without any previous knowledge was his most successful attempt at a "surprise." Taking her out to dinner is already so common that it is now only a "side dish" rather than an "entree" for such an occasion. Buying a ring for her can make her happy not because the ring is made of gold or is expensive, but because that would tell her that he knew what size of ring she was wearing, an indication that he "cared", as they put it. No matter whether it is "conventional" or full of novelty, these three occasions — one birthday for each and the wedding anniversary — become the most important days for Americans in terms of their emotional life.

Though Morris tries to keep his own individuality as a husband, he is totally in agreement with his wife in front of the children. If Anita says "no" to their four-year-old daughter Dana, and if Dana should turn to him and ask for the same thing, the answer is certainly "no," even if he would like her to answer "yes." The rule between the parents is: never disagree with each other in front of the children. In the family, it is considered impolite to break in while the others are having a conversation at the dinner table. Once their nine-year-old daughter Lauren was so excited about her school project that she forgot this family rule. As a result, she got a stern look from Daddy and an order to stop. Immediately, she was so upset that tears filled her eyes. She turned to Mommy with a pitiable expression, looking for sympathy. Mommy was of course sympathetic, but she didn't turn to Morris and try to disagree with him in favour of the daughter. Instead, she said to Lauren "you should wait for your turn." Finishing up the conversation with her husband in the shortest possible time, she turned to the daughter and said, "Now, what about your school project?"

I was present at the time and couldn't help thinking of a scene so common among the 4-2-1 Chinese family, in which the 1 "little emperor" is never wrong, since either one of the 2 (parents) would readily disagree with the other to "make the child feel good" or, in the unlikely event the two agree, one of the 4 (grandparents) is always there to "protect" the kid. "How can you be so unkind to the child," is the standard reproach sure to be heard from one of the grown-ups in favour of the little emperor when discipline is being enforced. No wonder the little emperor of China nowadays thinks it is the parents who are always wrong and that he can always have his own way.

One day, before Dana's birthday last April, Morris was fumbling through the mail of the day and said to Dana, "Look here, there is a birthday card for you". So saying, he proceeded to open it when the daughter protested: "But the card is for me!" Immediately, the father put down the card and said, "I'm sorry." Happily, Dana picked up the card and tore it open, making a mess of the envelope. Of course she was not yet able to read and had to give it back to Daddy. "What does it say?" she asked. It is not difficult to understand why Americans grow up to have that strong sense of privacy, both to have the right for themselves and to respect that of others. Children are treated equally even before they know what equality is. They are taught to have their own freedom and privacy so early that they take it for granted. To many Chinese, this birthday card episode is like making a mountain out of a molehill. To many Americans, on the other hand, it is incredible that parents should have the "right" to open the mail of grown-up children.

As a member of the Conservatives (the middle sector of the Jewish community, the most strict being the Orthodox and the least, the Reformed), Morris follows most of the rules of his religion. On Friday evenings, two candles are lit before dinner while the whole family sings their prayers in Hebrew. Once a year, in September, Morris fasts for 12 hours during Yom Kipper. The family never buys pork since it is against the teaching of the Torah. All pastries are hidden in the basement during Passover. Under Kosher dietary rules, chicken has to be killed in a particular way and dairy products must not be consumed together with meat. All these seem to indicate that Morris is religious, almost pious, except that his favourite food is spare ribs. Confirming my doubts about his religious sincerity, he said "never mind" after being warned that a Chinese moon cake I gave him to taste had ham in it. "Religion is just like a train, you get on board when you need it and get off when you don't."

For Morris, charity is part of his life. He contributes to the Synagogue, the school and the needy not simply to avoid taxes. It makes him feel good. This is perhaps one of the reasons why he went to work in a private law firm rather than for the government, which offers less money and freedom but more security. As a result, life is always a dilemma for him; either he is so busy making money that he has no time to spend it; or he is not busy but doesn't have enough money to enjoy his spare time. Such a dilemma is common among the majority of people who work in the private sector. In one of our conversations, I asked him about how he feels working for a private enterprise. "When you have just enough to do, you begin to worry that you may not have enough to do next; when you have less than enough, you begin to panic and start looking for other possibilities; when you have too much to do, you are happy but too tired to enjoy the happiness."

If there is a twig on the road, he, as well as many other educated Americans, would stop to pick it up and throw it to the roadside so it wouldn't be in the way. Many Chinese who wouldn't stop would ask "why me?" The Americans say "why not me?" Such is the lot of an individual in society. Morris goes further than that.

During one of his weekly trips to the grocery store, he was attracted by the design on one of the many cereal boxes. It was the Star of David (the symbol for the Synagogue), with a derogatory figure from a TV commercial. He didn't like to see the sacred symbol associated with such a figure and thought that perhaps many other Jewish people would share his feelings. So he told one of the clerks in the supermarket that he would like to have all the boxes with that design removed. The clerk didn't take him seriously but was polite enough to direct him to the manager, who promised that no new boxes would come in after those on the shelves were sold. Most people would take that generous promise and stop there, but not Morris. He wanted all of them removed immediately because he still considered it bad to have boxes with such a blasphemous design on the shelves for all people, especially children of Jewish families, to see. That was too much for the manager. He told Morris the issue involved the general-manager of the Giant store chain and the manufacturer. Morris, however, was not put off by that. He obtained the phone numbers and spent most of the next morning (as a lawyer, his time is as expensive as $100 per minute at work!) calling the general manager and the manufacturer, explaining to them his concern as a consumer.

To make a long story short, he got what he wanted and, sure enough, all the boxes with the offensive design were removed. Some Chinese would think that he was, as the proverb goes, "a dog chasing rats" — doing something outside his responsibility. But no, he was just an ordinary American doing his duty as a citizen. I asked him later what if they didn't do as he requested? After all, he was just one of millions of customers, and perhaps one of only hundreds who found it offensive. He told me he would certainly have made them do what he requested even if he had to sue them.

"What can you do in court for such a thing?" I asked.

"Oh, there are many ways, and the simplest of them would be to sue them for 'conflicting interest,' since Anita is a shareholder of the Giant chain."

He explained that if the chain did something against the interests of the shareholders, they could sue the chain. I was not quite sure he could have won the case had he gone that far. But I was sure that he would have fought until the issue was settled. Perhaps he saw it as a challenge, as many people do under such circumstances. But what touched me was his sense of responsibility as a citizen, the consciousness of one who cares. It seems to me that this is the strength of American society. Americans are not told, at least not as often as the Chinese people are, that they are the masters of the country and government officials just "people's servants." But they think so and act accordingly.

The Kerrs

Zhang Yun

IT was ten years ago, in the spring of 1978, that I was borrowed by the Chinese People's Association for Friendship with Foreign Countries to work as an interpreter for an American delegation called "Study Group on the Relations of Education and Work." This group of about 20 American educators was in China between April 25 and May 15. During the three weeks we visited a lot of schools, from a kindergarten in Guangzhou to Qinghua University in Beijing.

It was during this trip that I got to know the Kerrs. Clark Kerr was chairman of the Study Group and chairman of the Carnegie Council on Policy Studies in Higher Education. Mr. Kerr, whom I later called Clark, was easy-going, not very tall but quite well-built. He impressed me not because he was the head of the group, nor because he had fancy titles. His attraction lay in his natural smile and his seriousness in finding out about education in China. I think it was his smile that made him easy to get on with.

I still remember vividly a little experience in Guilin, a city famous for its beauty. People from all over the world come to see the unique hills, caves and the Lijiang River. But the study group also wanted to see a school. That morning we were at Guilin High School and students were having their classes. When we visited a math class the principal was going to tell the teacher to stop for a while in order to welcome the guests but Mr. Kerr smiled and shook his head, telling the teacher it wasn't necessary. This way, the group was able to visit several classes without disturbing the teachers too much.

I also admired his attitude towards the subjects he was studying. I was interpreting for the group when we visited a nursery in Guangzhou. The head of the nursery was talking about how they educated the three- and four-year olds. I found her introduction uninteresting. She was even telling the "foreign friends" how they taught the little ones to learn Marxism-Leninism and Mao Zedong Thought and how they taught them to serve the people. She went on and on.... I found it really dull and boring and didn't want to translate all this into English. But Mr. Kerr listened attentively. He later asked questions about teacher training and other questions.

Mrs. Kerr also had questions. She was a community leader in her area. Her major interest and experience was in gardening and outdoor recreation facilities. She was a good gardener herself, who knew countless names of plants and flowers. She asked about gardening in China including indoor plants. We talked about flowers and trees and I learned a great deal from her. She especially loved the sub-tropical plants in Guangzhou and the shapely trees that lined the streets in Nanjing. She was tall and full of life but her legs were sometimes not very strong.

When I was in Minnesota in 1984, I got a letter from Mr. Kerr. He said he had learned from Mr. Perkins, another member of the study group with whom I'd stayed in touch, that I was in the U.S. Among other things, he said, that if I visited San Francisco I was welcome to stay at his home.

In September 1985, two Chinese visiting scholars and I were planning a trip to the US west coast and wanted to stay in San Francisco for a couple of days. I remembered Mr. Kerr's letter and decided to write him to see whether it was possible for us to stay at his place. Within a few days, I got a call from his secretary telling me Mr. Kerr had got my letter and he wanted us to stay with him.

Our Greyhound bus arrived at the Berkeley bus station in the afternoon. We were very much charmed by the scenery between Mount Shasta city and Berkeley, but we were now a little worried because I knew Mr. Kerr was a busy man and I couldn't be too sure whether he was home at the time. His house was at El Cerrito, to the north of Berkeley, but we didn't know how to get there.

Like many other Greyhound bus stations, this one was situated close to the downtown area with lots of people moving around. I found a telephone and called Mr. Kerr. A familiar voice came on the other end of the line. It had been seven years since our last meeting, but instantly I could tell it was him.

He told me it would take him half an hour to get to the bus station. "Please wait."

In thirty minutes, I saw Mr. Kerr driving his car. He stopped, got out, shook hands with us and smiled — the smile I had liked. He told us he would like to show us his school on the way to his home. He had good reason to call the University of California at Berkeley *his* school. He was Berkeley's first chancellor in 1952, and was the Univeristy's twelfth president in 1958. During his ten years as president of the univeristy, it gained its fame and developed very fast. It was considered to be the nation's most distinguished university in terms of faculty quality. No wonder he loved the school dearly. He stopped his car a few times to show us different buildings, including some he himself had helped build when he was president. His face glowed with pride when he pointed out different corners of the school, very much like a gardener showing others the rich flowers and fruits in his garden. It was certainly a remarkable university. Although we were seeing it during the summer vacation, I could imagine how busy and crowded the place could be when school started again.

Huang, one of the scholars in our team of three, wanted to see a friend of his at the university and said he would meet us the following day. So we dropped him off and Mr. Kerr drove us to his house at El Cerrito.

Mrs. Kerr was waiting for us. She had prepared rooms for all of us to stay in and she had cooked a wonderful meal, too. It was an attractive white house with a swimming pool at the back and a lot of lemon trees. Mrs. Kerr told me they had fresh lemon all year round. Inside the house was a big room with windows on all sides and plants and flowers hanging down from the walls. Now I knew Kay was a good gardener. Then I went out of the room to the front of the house. At once I was caught by the beauty of the scene — the blue ocean and the enchanting Golden Gate Bridge in the distance. The house was towering over the bay. Kay was now calling us to have dinner. We came into the dining room to the long table. The aroma of the food was inviting — we were hungry by now. But just as we were going to eat, the telephone began to ring. Clark told me, "It's your friend." (I didn't know when, but I had begun to address Mr. Kerr as Clark.) Yes, it was Huang calling. He told me his friend had left for another place and he wanted to come over to Clark's place but he didn't know how. I told him the address and suggested that he should take a bus to come. Clark asked me what was the matter and I told him Huang's problem. He asked me to hand him the phone and told Huang, "I'll pick you up. Tell me where you are. OK, just stay where you are. I'll be there soon." He left the table and made for his car. We waited for another forty minutes before we had our dinner. I grew a little uneasy because I felt we had been too much trouble for Clark, who was a respected educator and economist, a person who had a lot of important things to do. His time was precious. But he came back with Huang smiling. We enjoyed the food enormously, not only because the beef, ham, salad, soup, and fruits were delicious, but also because by now everybody was really hungry.

We were chatting while eating, talking about China, about our experiences in the U.S., about Clark's expanding family — his daughter, who was staying with them at the moment, was expecting a second child. At one point, when we were talking about the University of California and the University of Minnesota, Clark said he knew how to get the best professors from all over the country for the U of C. Jokingly, he said he would pick up the phone and call a famous professor of the University of Minnesota during the coldest period of winter, asking him: "How's the weather there in Minnesota?" Minnesota was known for its harsh winter. The snow could be a few feet deep and it never seemed to melt away. "I was never mistaken about the answer. It would be something like: 'Well, it is awful!' Then I would tell him: 'You know it's just beautiful here! The sun is shining brightly and it's green outside the house. We don't see a flake of snow. Why don't you come and teach in Berkeley?" He told us the most important thing for a unviersity was to have the best professors. He had managed to get quite a few first class professors from other schools just like this.

That night we slept very well. The next morning I got up early because I wanted to have a good look at the sea. I rushed outside the house and came into the garden. Instantly, I was moved by the charm of the scene. The morning sun was just coming up. It sent its light over the blue ocean, making it look bluer than ever. On the left was the Oakland Bridge; on the right, the Golden Gate Bridge. They looked enchanting — at that moment the mist had just lifted. Buildings both in San Francisco and in Oakland looked like white marble, very much like terraces of countless white boxes. I looked around myself and saw I was surrounded by cacti in Kay's garden. Some were small and delicate, but many were huge. I still remember a giant spider-shaped cactus with green pointed leaves rimmed with yellow. Some tall ones had red fluffy flowers. I was like Alice in Wonderland.

I was called back to reality by the sound of an engine. It was Clark driving a small tractor. He was wearing a white, red and black check shirt and a pair of baggy pants that had some dots of mud on them. Obviously, he had been working. In the check shirt and in the morning sun, he looked fresh and full of energy. People would take him for a workman rather than an educator or a scholar. When he drove up to me, he smiled and said: "Morning. Did you sleep well?" I told him I had. But I was surprised to see him driving a tractor. He told me he was helping prepare a spot to put up a building for his daughter, on the lower left side of the house. By this time another Chinese scholar, Zhou, had come out of the house and joined us. He took a couple of pictures for Clark and me, with the bay and Golden Gate as the background.

Since Clark was busy that day, Kay offered to drive us to see San Francisco. But first we stopped at a waste-collection place where we saw half a dozen large garbage containers. Kay told us that now wastes of different kinds — such as paper, bottles, cans, etc.— were put into separate plastic bags and deposited here in different containers so they could be recycled. On the way Kay told us about her efforts to preserve the quality of life in the region. She and people like her had stopped landowners from carrying out plans that would have resulted in polluting the area and been able to save the bay for 25 years. I admired her spirit and determination.

Our favourite spot, as well as Kay's, was the Golden Gate Bridge. It perfectly combines the natural and man-made beauty. The two hills were linked by the immense orange-coloured suspension bridge, cutting the blue ocean into two parts. The ocean, the hills, the cities in the distance, the Oakland Bridge ... all were bathed in the sun. Kay pointed to the east. We saw, across the bay, the hilly place where the Kerr house stood. Kay and others had good reason to guard the loveliness of the area.

That was my experience with the Kerrs in 1985. I hear from them now and then, the two gardeners — Clark and Kay. I am very happy to have learned that a part of the Berkeley Campus was dedicated to Clark as "Clark Kerr Campus" on November 13, 1986. Excerpts from the dedication go like this:

"Clark Kerr is a Cal aluminus (Ph.D. 1939) and faculty member who became Berkeley's first chancellor in 1952 and the University's 12th President in 1958.

"His leadership and outstanding record as a

scholar and teacher have earned him international respect in two fields — higher education and industrial relations.... He built a strong record of accomplishment, including the design and funding of the Student Center and the launching of major expansion for student housing. He also strengthened student government, and he liberalized rules for political expression (which won him the 1964 Alexander Meiklejohn Award for Contributions to Academic Freedom).

"During Kerr's years as UC President (1958-67), Berkeley came to be rated as the nation's most distinguished university in terms of faculty quality; three new campuses — Irvine, Santa Cruz and San Diego — were developed; and the Master Plan for Higher Education in California was prepared....

"Kerr helped the Carnegie Commission on Higher Education 1967-69.... Polls during those years rated Kerr as 'the most influential person in the field of education.' Now President Emeritus of UC and Professor Emeritus of Economics and Industrial Relations at Berkeley,... Berkeley has honored him with the faculty's Clark Kerr Medal and the Kerr Room of the Faculty Club — and now most fittingly, with the naming of the Clark Kerr Campus."

Clark Kerr is a big name in US education. Many of my American professors have confirmed that. But the Clark Kerr I know is the one who visited China in 1978, the one who drove the three of us to his home, and the one who was driving a tractor with mud on his pants.

Going to Court in the United States

Fan Qi

IT'S over a year since I came to study in the United States. During this period, although I was living off-campus, I knew very little of real American society, since I kept myself busy with studies and most of my acquaintances were students.

But some months ago I was injured in a car accident, which gave me a chance to know a little more of America because after the accident I had to see a doctor — and go to court.

Immediately after the accident, my roommate called a doctor for me on his own initiative. I was very moved and determined to repay him for his kindness after my recovery. So days later when he asked me to pay him $200 for what he had done I was astounded. He had good reason to charge me, he said. He had helped me find a good doctor; without the doctor a good lawyer could not be recommended, and without a good lawyer it would be difficult for me to get compensation.

He also offered to buy medicine for me, which was politely declined at first. But at his insistence and due to the fact that I could not go myself because of the injury, I had to give in. When I got the medicine, however, I found something wrong. With over $50 he had bought pain-killers, but there were only seventeen tablets in the box! A standard pack should contain an even number of pills. When asked to explain, he told me he had taken some of the pills because he was a drug addict and needed the pain-killers, too. What is more, the rest disappeared before I had consumed half of them. No doubt, he had taken them when he moved out.

Because of my injury, my classmates would take me to see the doctor by car. It took 40 minutes. Every time, I would have to wait about 20 minutes and then be received by the nurse for about half an hour. Later I found the doctor saw two or three patients at the same time. He would often stop treating one to see another who had more pain at that moment. Yet he charged me $115 each time. Every time when I went to see him I would dream of "Landlord Zhou" (a cruel exploiter in a Chinese story) that night. The final examination report was only one page and ten lines, for which he charged me $215.

My lawyer was almost a swindler. Except for the first meeting during which he was all smiles, he avoided seeing me at all after I retained his services. As he knew the other party bore the entire liability in my case he simply waited to collect his fee. Seeing how irresponsible he was, I dismissed him. However, he listed his services in six pages and charged me $770. I could hardly believe this open extortion.

After dismissing the lawyer, I had to deal with the insurance company by myself for compensation. Due to my inexperience, I told them the date of my departure from America. Knowing I did not have enough time for negotiation, they played for time, about which I could do nothing.

My experiences after the accident taught me two things about America: firstly, in a country like America with a highly developed material civilization, the idea that "money is almighty" is an objective reality. For money, people can disregard friendship, a sense of honour or even professional morality. Secondly, foreigners (including minorities in the United States) are still discriminated against. For me it was natural to suffer losses since I did not know much about American laws and lacked experience.

I want my personal experiences to be a warning: when we talk about America we should see both its good and bad sides. In fact, what happened to me is only a trivial experience. To live in the real America one would find the country is not the paradise it is commonly imagined.

Mr. Blume

Zhang Yun

MR. Blume was my landlord for two years during my stay in Minnesota. He was also a good friend and a father figure, the person I saw almost daily when I was there.

Before I went to Minnesota, a friend had arranged for me to rent a room from Mr. Blume. She told me the Blumes were very friendly to the Chinese. At about dusk on March 10, 1984, I arrived at Minneapolis airport. An American couple, Mr. and Mrs. Egley had volunteered to meet me at the airport and they drove me to 2464 Como Avenue St. Paul — Mr. Blume's house. It was winter and still quite cold in Minnesota — the ground was covered with snow. I felt rather nervous, a natural response to this strange, new city.

I saw a three-story grey house, quite big compared with other houses nearby. I knocked at the door. Out came a round-faced man about 70. I knew at once this was Mr. Blume. I said good-bye to the Egleys and went inside. Mr. Blume reached out his hands and took my big suitcase, which was too heavy for me to carry. It was the first time that I noticed his strong hands. He led me to my room on the second floor, where I found an old-fashioned oak bed and clean bedding, a chest of drawers, a desk, bookshelves and a colour TV set. He smiled and told me to sleep well. I was far away from home now and was feeling miserably lonely, but I had this new home and the smile of Mr. Blume. A flood of warmth hit me from the radiator. The room was very well heated.

I didn't get up until well after noon because I had not been able to fall asleep until the morning. After eating breakfast prepared by Gao, a Chinese girl living in another room on the second floor, Mr. Blume offered to drive me to a supermarket. Gao told me he drove his three Chinese boarders to the market every other week. And whenever we needed anything, he would help us buy it.

I lost count of how many times Mr. Blume drove us to the supermarket, to other stores and shops. He even drove me to the airport, to the Greyhound bus station when I was going to visit my friends in other parts of the country and he picked me up from the airport when I was coming home. He did this voluntarily and never charged me anything. It was through the rides that I got to know him better because we were always chatting on the way. He was very frank, willing to tell us about himself.

"I don't like those young people who throw away their money like paper," he said. "They should know the value of living a serious life. It's a crime to waste anything. When I was thirteen years old, we had nothing to eat at home. My family was literally starving. I was looking in the garbage for food. Once when I was really hungry, I stole a couple of bottles of milk and picked a few corncobs. I hated to do that. I knew it was not right, but we were starving."

He told me that because of poor nutrition he didn't grow as tall as he should have. He was a small and thin boy.

But he grew into a handsome young man and married a pretty girl, now Mrs. Blume. He once showed us some of his old black-and-white pictures. We saw a handsome, slim young soldier. He had been a worker when he joined the U.S. Army during the Second World War. He fought against the Germans in North Africa, where he suffered a bullet wound in the knee. He came home, married his girl and started a family of his own. He had two daughters and a son. He had bought this house for his growing family.

It was because of his wounded knee that he retired early from his job as a machine worker. One day he showed us the scar. His leg was weak as a result of the wound and he found it hard to walk for long. It was difficult for him in winter to shovel snow, which could be very heavy.

That was why we three Chinese students decided to help whenever it snowed. I enjoyed doing that for him because it felt good to do something in return for his kindness, and it was good exercise as well. Often he would join us. Once or twice when it had snowed heavily, we would all end up covered with snow. Mr. Blume, with his hat and his blue pullover looked exactly like a snowman. We would tease him and laugh. He said he must pay us for helping him but we would tell him we had volunteered. Then he would say, "That won't do! That won't do!" And later he would always find a way to "make it up," either by buying us big pieces of meat, or fruits and vegetables. He also cooked good bean soup. Every time the delicious aroma came up to my room from his kitchen, I knew I would soon be enjoying a bowl. My mouth waters even today, over two years since I left his house, when I think of the flavour.

We had other gifts from Mr. Blume as well. The regular ones were fish and maple syrup. He had a lot of hobbies including making articles with wood. He once offered to give me a twiller to hang in front of my house in China, but I told him I didn't have a house and that it would be better for him to sell it for some money. He would drive all the way to Lake Michigan a few times every year to fish for salmon and trout. He took me to his trailer and showed me everything inside: the place he kept his ice box, the bed, the oven where he cooked his meals, etc. Every time he came back from the lake he would give us each some fish. And we knew we would have smoked fish as well because he had a smokehouse in the back yard. It took a lot of time, usually eight to nine hours; it also took a special skill. It needed a certain type of wood cut into tiny bits. No wonder it had a unique flavour. We would keep the fish in the fridge in our big kitchen for several days before we could finish it.

Mr. Blume also had a cabin by a lake in Northern

Minnesota. Every year he went there to make maple syrup. It was hard work. He would go to the forest and make countless cuts on maple trunks to get the sap and then he would boil it until it was as thick as paste. The result was very sweet. He always had a bottle for me, and Mrs. Blume taught me how to make pancakes to eat with the syrup.

Every time Mr. Blume was fishing or making maple syrup, he had to be away from home for a few days. And Mrs. Blume was still working in a factory. I would then be asked to look after the house and his two dogs when I was at home. The little white dog, Mr. Blume's best friend, was called Muffin; the small black one was Carsia. Muffin was a lively and intelligent dog. Mr. Blume loved him very much. For Muffin's haircut, Mr. Blume would drive all the way to his son's home asking him for help. Mr. Blume also studied how to keep the dogs in better health. For example, he gave them rice to eat. "Rice has less fat," he told me. "Since they are growing old, I have to watch out for them."

Muffin was very much like a child. When Mr. Blume was away he would cry and cry. It was my duty to calm him down. I could get him to stop crying for a while but then he would start again. Sometimes I would go down to Mr. Blume's living room to do my lessons in order to keep Muffin company. Carsia was a quieter dog. She wouldn't make a noise unless Muffin started crying. Then they would begin a duet.

As soon as Mr. Blume's car could be heard coming home, Muffin would jump to the windowsill and start barking happily. I always liked the scene when Mr. Blume opened the door. Muffin would jump and cry excitedly. Mr. Blume once told me he would call Muffin "Muffin Blume," and he wanted to have him buried beside him when the time came. He said he owed a lot to Muffin. It was because of the dog that the house was never robbed. I also liked the scene of Mr. Blume lying on his big sofa watching TV with Muffin sitting at his side chewing his bone. It was very harmonious.

Mr. Blume chose rice for Muffin and Carsia yet he himself didn't like it. But he did worry about his weight. He had grown pretty heavy and he was afraid that his weak legs wouldn't be able to carry him. Often he would touch his pot-belly with his strong hands and say: "I would like to get rid of it." But it was difficult for a person with good appetite to do so. He loved "junk food" and ate ice cream while watching TV. I also love Minnesota ice cream and know how difficult it is to resist the temptation. He told me he knew these junk foods were not healthy but he couldn't help himself. On our way shopping I sometimes saw him entering a drug store to buy all kinds of drugs to curb his appetite. I understood his weight was a real headache.

One day, I smelled the strong odour of cigarettes on the stairway. I knew he was smoking when I first got to the house but then both Mrs. Blume and I managed to convince him to quit. We were very glad he had given it up but now, after many months, he was smoking again. Coming back home from the University of Minnesota one afternoon, I went to his living room and found an ashtray full of cigarette butts and Mr. Blume lying in his big sofa watching a football game on the TV with a cigarette between his fingers.

"Why are you smoking again, Mr. Blume?"

"It's the only way to stop my appetite. When I begin to smoke, I am able to cut down my food, and then I would lose a few pounds."

It turned out to be true. After a period of time, he told me with a smile that he had lost five pounds. I then suggested that it was time for him to quit smoking again. He did quit for a while but he then regained the five pounds. So he was smoking again to lose the weight. It was the first time in my life that I had learned it was such a torture to keep from putting on weight and that smoking was a way of slimming. I don't know whether he is still smoking or not, but I wish he could find a better way.

It was hard for Mr. Blume to lose weight but it was easy for him to shop. He could always get things at more reasonable prices than others. One afternoon coming home from school I was caught in a light rain. I rushed into the front porch and found Mr. Blume and Muffin sitting there.

"Yan, you know what? I bought a camera from a yard sale." He always called me "Yan" because "Yun" is very difficult for Americans to pronounce. I looked at the camera. It was quite new but of an old style.

"How much did you pay for it?"

"Guess."

I told him I couldn't. He told me then, proudly,

that he paid only $2.

"The boy asked for five; I said two, and he let me have it for two."

To find out whether the $2 camera worked, Mr. Blume snapped a picture of me sitting on the big sofa with Muffin in my lap. The picture came out perfectly and I now have it on my bookshelf. The big brown sofa, white Muffin and the rain drops on my light-blue shirt are all reminders of my life in Mr. Blume's house.

Later, he used the same camera to take other pictures. Some were of his house covered with snow; some were of his wife and the three of us, his "Chinese girls," mowing the lawn and trimming the bushes. But the most unforgettable pictures were those of Mr. Blume wearing his old army helmet.

It was a beautiful morning in fall. Liu, another Chinese student living on the second floor, and I went down to have a chat with Mr. Blume. I had always enjoyed chatting with him. Once when the professor I was working with was teaching Tennessee Williams' *A Streetcar Named Desire*, I had asked Mr. Blume to tell me what poker is like because the central symbol of the play is a poker game. He told me the rules and we played a few games together. In the end he took out a new set of cards and gave it to me. I still have it today.

When Liu and I were in his living room, he was happy to have us with him. This time Liu suggested that Mr. Blume show us the uniform he had worn in the army. He went to his room and came out with a helmet and a khaki uniform. We wanted him to put them on so that we could take a picture for him. The helmet suited him very well but the khaki jacket could only cover half of his body, the front part of him, the pot-belly, stuck out in a funny way. We all laughed. He took it off and said it might suit us. He was right. The jacket suited both of us nicely. We also tried the helmet but it was definitely too large. Mr. Blume said he would like to take some pictures for us. We liked the idea and I suggested that we should go out because it was a beautiful fall morning. The great oak in front of the house was turning yellow; the few maple trees were touched with red; the bushes on the other side of the road were already as red as fire. The sky was sea-blue with some white clouds. It was the best time to take pictures and I wanted to save all this in my memory. We took quite a few photos: Mr. Blume and Liu, Mr. Blume and Muffin, Liu and me, Mr. Blume and me and Muffin.... Our good neighbour Mrs. Smith was working on her lawn. We also took a few with her. Later Mr. Blume gave us each a set of the pictures. I can't help laughing whenever I look at Mr. Blume smiling at me under that helmet of his, and look at myself in his American khaki uniform with Muffin in my arms.

Mr. Blume also has something to remind him of his Chinese girls besides his pictures. He had a Chinese "Corner" in his living room where he kept all kinds of gifts from the several generations of Chinese girls who had stayed with him. Most of them were Christmas gifts, such as a carved lacquer case, a cork patchwork of trees and houses, a

Chinese pagoda, a sandalwood fan, a woven-silk landscape, etc. Every Christmas Eve, each of us would also be given a box of gifts wrapped in colourful paper by Mrs. Blume.

Mr. Blume once told me he would like to make his house a home for Chinese girls if he could get enough of them. He let the third floor to two Amercian girls. He said these two were nice but he'd had an unhappy experience with two others. One night they left without saying good-bye and without paying that month's rent. It was from then on that Mr. Blume started to ask for a deposit for his rooms. But with me, he was very kind. I didn't pay either the rent or the deposit the first month I was there. I told him I would pay when I got my very first pay check from the University of Minnesota. He trusted me and let me have the room, and use of the kitchen with all the necessary utensils. He even let me use the washing machine and dryer in the basement free of charge. He was good to all of the girls. I remember how worried Yuan was after she had put too many clothes into the washing machine and it broke down. She didn't sleep well that night because it would be expensive for her to buy a new one and there would be a lot of inconvenience for the others. But Mr. Blume, instead of getting angry, told her to be more careful in the future. He said the machine was getting old anyway and it was time for him to buy another one. The following day he went out and bought a new washing machine. Mrs. Blume called all of us together to tell us how to use it.

It is over two years since I left Minnesota, but the memories of Mr. Blume are still fresh. I found it hard to say good-bye to him. He drove me to the airport. His strong hands again carried my suitcases. Tears were in my eyes — I could no longer hear him calling me "Yan," or "Kiddo."

Service Attitudes in the U.S.

Chen Jing

AMERICANS working in the service trades display the warmth of their country's people. Shops and restaurants are run by individuals. Once you walk into these shops you will find it embarrassing to leave without buying something. Shop assistants wait on customers politely, helping to select articles without tiring of the customers' questions and choices.

Once I touched a skirt for a look and the assistant immediately came over. She greeted me and, after exchanging a few words, bombarded me with information about where the skirt was made, its material and style. Without waiting for a response, she began to take my measurements with a ruler. Then she selected a pink silk skirt and enthusiastically persuaded me to try it on. I had no choice but to do so. Having examined me for a while, she said: "You look beautiful in this skirt. You are tall and slender. This skirt fits you well." Hearing her praise, I wanted to buy it. But when I saw it cost $180, I said: "I think it is too expensive." I had hardly finished my words when she took out two other skirts of a similar style: "These two skirts are made of cotton. They feel soft and they are cheap. You will surely like them." Finding no way to refuse, I bought one at last.

Another time in New York, when I entered a photographic equipment store, I was warmly received by a middle-aged man. With a kind and courteous attitude he introduced to me all the electrical appliances in the store as if enumerating his family valuables. Then he asked: "What would you like to buy, Miss?" Still remembering the experience last time, I answered: "Thank you, I just want to have a look," not showing my real intention to buy a 135 camera. My words froze his facial expression. He turned around to greet other customers. But he reappeared beside me as if he had come out of the ground the moment I stood in front of a camera. He put the camera in my hands, smiling broadly. Since I didn't have much knowledge about cameras, I asked him: "Can I put 135 film into this camera?" He answered immediately: "Yes, both 135 film and 120 film can be used in this camera. This camera is the latest product." "What type of battery does the flash need?" In reply he asked: "What type of battery is used in your country?" "Usually No. 5." "Wonderful, the camera also uses No. 5. You will like it, I assure you." Satisfied after I bought this camera, he saw me to the door, smiling "Welcome again."

Though the camera later worked well, it turned out after I returned home that only 110 film and No. 8 batteries could be used in it.

Americans from A to Z

Xie Shihao

AFTER more than four decades in the United States, I have not succeeded in learning all there is to know about Americans. Nonetheless, I would point out the following ABC.

A — Americans are Westerners.

B — Busy folks, whether blue- or brown-eyed.

C — Competition in business.

D — Dollars are an uncommonly common goal.

E — Enter and exit human relationships quickly.

F — Friendly to good friends.

G — 'Go-for-it' is a motto.

H — Hypertension goes with a high income and high living.

I — Impatience is a trait.

J — Jamboree may jeopardize your health.

K — Kiss and Ride, a sign in a subway.

L — Love means ALOHA in the generic sense.

M — 'Me-first' attitude.

N — Nosiness is tabooed.

O — Oops is an exclamation or interjection.

P — Penny wise and pound foolish in value judgments.

Q — Quest for influence.

R — Risk is the foundation of the firm.
S — Salesmanship is a benign tumour.
T — Teasing is a sign of being liked.
U — Unemployment breeds foreclosures.
V — Vulnerable to temptations.
W — Woo fame and fortune.
X — A movie classification for sex and violence.
Y — Yen for yen, the Japanese currency.
Z — Zest for fun and pleasure.

The Americans I Know:
Not Much Different from
Us Chinese

Shang Rongguang

W HEN I first arrived at New York's Kennedy airport in late August 1984, the first thing I wanted was to meet people from the Chinese Consulate. I was travelling with two companions, Shao Ping, a young man from Beijing's New World Press and Yang Nan, a young woman from the magazine *Chinese Literature*. As exchange students from a programme between the Foreign Language Publication and Distribution Administration and Illinois State University, we were on our way to attend school in the United States. Although we had been told that we could spend our first night in a hotel at the bureau's expense, I decided that would be a last resort. Taking a cab to a hotel the first night you arrive in New York? What a risk! Just think of the possibilities of robbery, rape, and other crimes you read about in *Time* and *Newsweek*, as well as numerous Chinese publications!

While one of us looked after our luggage, the other two watched the people criss-crossing the crowded terminal. I finally spotted a man holding a placard reading *Zhongguo Lingshiguan* (Chinese Consulate).

Once inside the consulate's minibus, I realized all my worries had been unnecessary. More than half of the passengers on the CAAC flight from Beijing were Chinese, and many were going to the consulate. There were seven minibuses — besides cars for distinguished officials — and all were full.

But the scene outside reminded me that I was on foreign soil. I saw more cars on the highway from airport to New York than I had ever seen in my whole life. The opposing lanes of dense traffic were like two dragons — one white, the other red — prowling towards each other.

"Ah, that's America, the prosperous capitalist country!" I told myself. "But there must be another side — its declining morality and rotten culture," I had read about in books by domestic and Western authors.

As the bus neared the consulate in mid-Manhattan, my expectations were soon satisfied. I was sure that 99 out of 100 Chinese would have been shocked to see a black prostitute wearing a nylon suit that made her look nude dancing in the street. Now and then, she would sway her hips towards the passersby while about 20 metres away a policeman stood by oblivious to her performance. "He must have closed at least one of his eyes," someone in the bus commented.

These first glimpses of America aroused my curiosity even more: what kind of people was I going to meet in the coming two years?

Normal! Normal!

I never expected that, two years later back in Beijing, when I was asked what I thought about Americans, I would respond, "They're normal, not much different from us Chinese."

This discovery came from my experiences in Normal, one of the twin-cities of Bloomington and Normal in central Illinois where Illinois State University is located. Surrounded by corn fields, life in this quiet, clean town was idyllic to me after growing up in Beijing. At first, I was excited about going back to school after many years of working, getting married, and raising children; I looked forward to attending courses and making new friends. However, within a couple of months, I was bored by life in Normal — there were no great museums, no theatres, and scarcely any chances to go sightseeing if you didn't have a car. Normal was filled with "normal" people.

I didn't think much about the word "normal" when I first heard some housewives introduce themselves as "normal" at a meeting of host families. "I'm from Normal, and I'm normal: I have one husband, two children — one girl and one boy..." they would say.

It was only after I had met more Americans that I understood the real meaning of the word "normal" and why the Normal people appreciated it so much — it reflected the common values of family, friendship, and love shared by all peoples, Americans and Chinese, despite their different cultural backgrounds and political systems.

The Finkbiners

I stayed with William and Millie Finkbiner during the 1984 Christmas vacation.

I needed a place to stay during the holidays because the school dorm would be closed. Marilyn, the foreign students' activities coodinator, gave me a slip of paper with a name and phone number on it. "Call this lady," she told me. "She wants to invite a foreign student to stay at their house for Christmas." I called, and about 20 minutes later Millie Finkbiner appeared in the lobby of my dorm.

Millie was a tall, energetic woman in her 50s. She took me to a nearby restaurant where I had a cup of coffee with the rest of the family — Bill Finkbiner, her husband, and Shauna, her daughter by a former marriage. When Shauna went back to her job as a hairdresser the Finkbiners drove me to their office. They ran a gas station construction and maintenance company.

In the office, I met Betty Wiser, their secretary. We shook hands and Betty gave me a properly restrained polite smile. But when she heard that I was from the People's Republic of China she was so shocked that her hand trembled in mine. Her eyes widened and she murmured, "So you're a Communist!" I knew what she meant by "Communist" since she was old enough to remember the McCarthy period. But I was not upset. There was no doubt that I was the first Chinese Communist she had ever seen.

We didn't talk much that day. But when I wrote her name in Chinese as *Beidi*, and told her "it means bud, so you're a bud which is going to blossom," she burst into hearty laughter. Betty later gave me a whole packet of MacDonald's coupons as a Christmas gift because she knew that there were no dinners served in the school cafeteria on Sundays.

The other person I met in the office was Bob, who owned an electrical equipment company and shared the same office building with the Finkbiners. Bob was known as the silent type, but he greeted me warmly and gave me a green ballpoint pen as a present. I told him I liked the pen especially because the green colour implies life and peace. He gave me an embarrassed smile and left.

I learned later that Bob had fought in the Korean War. That reminded me of my uncle, who had been an officer in the Chinese People's Volunteers during that conflict. I remembered hearing him talking about their heroic fighting against the U.S. invaders. I always admired the dozens of merit medals that glittered on his chest, and never thought that one day I would be talking face to face with an American soldier who had fought on the opposite side.

Hospitality: Different Style

Like us Chinese, the Americans are hospitable. But they show their hospitality in a totally different way. For example, when a Chinese family has a house guest, especially a close relative or a friend from far away, like a foreigner, the guest automatically becomes the focus of the whole family's attention. The hosts treat their guest with the best food they can afford and tailor the family menu to their guest's taste. Sometimes either the host or hostess asks for leave from work to take their guest sightseeing.

Americans, however, welcome their guests by taking them in as one of themselves, part of the family, without giving them any special attention. Westerners may feel at home with this, but Orientals are not used to it and may misinterpret it as neglect.

A Thai girl once complained to me that her Christmas vacation in Washington D.C. was not interesting and that she would never again choose a host family for a vacation.

"What happened?" I asked.

"Nothing. I just think I was probably not welcome."

"But how?"

"They didn't care much about me. When I said I would like to go to some museum, they said, 'OK, you go ahead.' And they did whatever they'd planned, and paid no attention to my existence."

One example she gave was that once the whole family was going skating and she went with them out of politeness. "I never did ice skating in Thailand, and I don't like it. As a visitor and a foreign student, I'd like to see more of the city," she said.

Her hosts, though kind, probably never thought about this aspect of the Oriental psyche. They might even have been surprised to learn that the Thai girl didn't want to go skating with them. "Why did she go?" they would ask.

I had a similar experience with the Finkbiners. They were always busy with work, and none of them spent even half a day with me. When they went to the office, they just asked me to choose between going with them and staying home. Nevertheless, behind that seemingly casual hospitality, I saw their very thoughtful hearts. They took me to Chinese restaurants; at home, they always told me I didn't need to eat things I didn't like; when they had business in Springfield, they remembered to take me to Lincoln's home.... Above all, they trusted me with their house. Can you imagine a Chinese family trusting their home to a foreigner who is neither a relative nor an old friend, but a stranger?

My First Christmas

The Christmas of 1984 was the first I ever celebrated and it might also have been the saddest had it not been for the Finkbiners.

I was embraced in the merry Christmas atmosphere of people decorating their houses with coloured lights and red and green wreaths, preparing gifts, and visiting friends. But when Christmas Eve drew close, I fell into a depression all of a sudden, thinking about my husband in Africa and my two teenage girls in Beijing. Afraid that my misery might hurt others, I tried hard to suppress my feelings and join the rest of the family in the Christmas Eve celebration.

However, once I was sitting by the Christmas tree and the fireplace, my loneliness and sadness gradually dissipated. Santa Claus came to me as well. I became part of the family when we unwrapped gifts. There were so many for me — a nightgown, a sweater, perfume, a book... it was not only the Finkbiner family who presented me with all kinds of gifts — their friends who shared the season's happiness with them that night gave me things as well. When I finally took a necklace cast with the big bronze Chinese character of *shou* (longevity) out of the stocking that hung on the fireplace, I could no longer hide my excitement as Chinese are supposed to. I put on the necklace and rushed over to Bill and Millie and gave them a deep bow. "Thank you Dad, thank you Mom," I choked. Tears rolled down my cheeks. "You're welcome, darling. You're our daughter and we wish you happiness and longevity," said Millie, whose eyes also filled with happy tears.

How did they learn that the best traditional Chinese wish for the new year is longevity?

Unfeeling, or Thoughtful

I had heard that Americans were casual and even unfeeling. But what I saw that Christmas was just the opposite: they care as much about their relatives and friends as the Chinese do. Exchanging gifts during Christmas is often thought of as a tradition or a ceremonial custom. In fact, it's a good opportunity for people to show their feelings for one another. The gifts may be small and inexpensive, but every one was carefully chosen to meet the recipients' needs or wishes. Berry, a hairdresser at the Finkbiners' beauty shop, got a watch from his bosses because they knew that his old one had broken a few days before Christmas; Betty, who lived alone and had been suffering from a backache, received an electric blanket which she said was "almost as good as a man in bed."

I remember that on Christmas morning, when the whole family was going out for breakfast, Shauna suddenly excused herself and went back to her bedroom, saying she would join us at the restaurant. She arrived with a mysterious smile on her face. When we returned home, a huge package had appeared under the Christmas tree. The card read: "To Millie, Happy Christmas! From Bill." Millie opened it and cried, "A microwave oven! Just what I've dreamed of!" I realized then why Shauna had been late for breakfast and what a game the stepfather and daughter had played with the mother.

Another seemingly trivial episode also demonstrated that it is wrong to stereotype Americans as careless and frivolous.

Millie's oldest daughter, Julie, lived with her family in Minnesota. She often talked on the phone with her mother and stepfather. One day, Julie told her mother she'd had a problem with the down overcoat they had given her for Christmas the previous year: all the feathers had fallen down to the hem, leaving most of the upper part empty.

"Why don't you take it back to the store and get the money back?" her mother suggested.

"I did," the daughter replied. "But the clerk told me that I could only get one-third of the money back because they can't send the coat back to the factory."

"Why not?"

"It was made in China."

I felt like begging their pardon, hearing "China" mentioned this way. My face flushed, and I bowed my head. I wished I were somewhere else!

I was just wondering how those American eyes would be looking at me when I heard Bill say kindly, "This could happen in any country. There are bad products here too." The words were simple, but what a thoughtful, sensitive spirit they showed!

Dissimilarities

Despite the common feelings I shared with the Finkbiners, I don't deny there are great dissimilarities between Americans and Chinese in customs and psychology. The fact is, when we overemphasize the differences based on cultural and political factors, we often neglect the very delicate feelings harboured deep in the heart. There was at least one thing that I myself could have done better if I had been aware of these subtleties.

I received two sweaters from the Finkbiners as Christmas gifts. The light green one was said to have been chosen by Bill because he thought the colour complemented my black hair. I liked both of them, wrapped them up carefully, and put them into my suitcase: my Chinese mind told me that gifts from friends are more for memory than for practical use and should be preserved. I hoped that when I came back to China and showed the gifts to my friends and relatives, they would be as new as when I had received them.

On Christmas day, I wore a sweater I had brought with me from home. In the afternoon, Millie told me it seemed too small, and there was a note of unhappiness in her tone. Only then did I notice that Shauna was wearing the new sweater her sister had given her, Berry was wearing his new watch and Terry had on his new shirt, a gift from his girlfriend. What different ways people express their respect and gratitude for friendship or love!

The Chinese like to talk about *shanshi shan-zhong* (good beginnings and good endings). When you have a house guest, it means showing perfect hospitality. But that's not enough. Usually, when guests are leaving, the host, and especially the hostess, say repeatedly that they don't want them to leave because the days they've spent together have been too short. They will try to persuade the guests to postpone their departure. This, in return, gives the guests an opportunity to express their thanks and gratitude for the hospitality.

But my departure from the Finkbiners' was not at all in the Chinese way. The morning my dorm reopened, they drove me back. As a guest, I wanted to say good-bye as early as possible because I didn't want to bother them any more. They had their reasons for agreeing -- they needed to do shopping and other things that Sunday, and Bill was going to watch a football game on TV that afternoon.

I understood that in a fast-paced society, everyone has a busy schedule and ceremonial politeness has to be omitted. Bill and Millie were as frank and pragmatic as the majority of the Americans. But, to my Chinese mind, it was still a pity -- it was too quick a departure, given the days and nights of good times we'd had together.

Oh, Those Little Gold Earrings

An account of the women's dormitory for foreign students

Wang Yongmei

W ITH mixed feelings of curiosity, excitement and uneasiness, I moved into room 340 in the small white building built specially for foreign students who study at Nanjing University. My roommate was a tall, sturdy American girl who, like other foreign students, was given a Chinese name -- Ge Xinya.

The first night we talked for quite a long time both in English and Chinese. The more we talked, the closer we felt to each other.

"My hometown is Franklin Lake in Pennsylvania," Ge Xinya said pointing to the map of America on the wall beside her bed. "It's a very beautiful small town with a population of about 150,000."

"Ah, that's interesting. My hometown, Yancheng, is also a small town with 120,000 people."

"When were you born?" she asked.

"On March 29, 1967," I replied.

"My God. What a happy coincidence! I was born on that day, too," she jumped for joy. "I was born at 1:00 pm. What about you?"

"At 4:00 pm. You are my sister then," I said feeling excited too.

"Our birthday is coming in about ten days. Let's celebrate it together then. Shall we?" she suggested.

"That's a good idea, right in our cosy room. That's settled then!" Both of us looked closer at each other smiling wholeheartedly.

It was late at night. Neither of us felt at all sleepy. She opened one of her suitcases and took out a photo album. "This is my father. This is my mother. This is my sister playing tennis with me, and this is me at a beach." She quietly turned the pages of the album and my eyes were busy jumping from one picture to another following her finger.

My eyes finally stopped at the last one she pointed to. She is gorgeous in a bikini, full of vitality and youthful beauty. I have no doubt that everyone who saw the picture admired her beautiful figure, except for those girls who were envious.

"Is this in California?" I asked.

"No, in Hawaii," she suddenly uttered in English.

I was at a loss. I quickly reached for the English and Chinese Dictionary beside me.

"Let's forget about it," she said in Chinese and smiled at me. Her pronunciation was not quite right so it sounded a little bit funny. She got up and showed me the place on the map.

"Hawaii, how come you don't know this?"

She hesitated and was surprised to find that I was so ignorant about it. It seemed that she was a geographer and I was a pupil.

"Oh, Hawaii!"

My goodness, a college student that can't understand this simple English word. What a shame! But I am a person who refuses to be left behind. In order to win a point or get even, I asked her in reply:

"Honolulu in Hawaii is well known. Dr. Sun Zhongshan, our revolutionary forerunner, once lived there. Don't you know this period of history?"

She obviously did not know who Dr. Sun Zhongshan (Dr. Sun Yat-sen) was so in her answer she mistook Dr. Sun Zhongshan for a mountain (*shan* means a mountain in Chinese).

She looked very much embarrassed. She had no alternative but to shrug her shoulders and say: "Let's forget about it." Then she laughed and covered herself with the quilt.

Well, my lovely and funny roommate, I finally got the best of you. And that night I slept deeply and soundly.

No and Thank You

It was only a very short period of time, but Ge Xinya made an unforgettable impression on me. Her blond hair and high-bridged nose along with a pair of black eyes combined Western frankness and Oriental gentleness. However, what most surprised me was that she was so sincere she sometimes appeared naive.

One Sunday morning we were chatting as usual while doing our washing and getting dressed.

"Mei Mei, you are so pretty, just like a rose," she said.

"What are you talking about? I am not as pretty as a rose at all, but a blade of grass." Although I said so, I felt very comfortable and quite pleased.

Upon hearing my words she acted differently. Her eyes suddenly grew bigger, looking puzzled. "Mei Mei, what you have just said is unfair," she said seriously. "You are really beautiful. Why must you depreciate yourself in that way?"

"Ge Xinya, you don't understand our Chinese customs," I smiled and explained to her. "When someone praises you, you should always make a few modest remarks."

"Oh, I see. When you hear someone's commendations, you always shake your head and say 'no, no'. But we Americans do just the opposite. We usually say 'Thank you' instead."

"Don't you think we Americans are modest?" she asked.

"No, I think you are very frank."

"That's true. I like to hear others' praises, especially when they say I am pretty. In college at home I was considered one of the prettiest girls and five boys fell in love with me," she said to me without feeling ashamed.

Then she continued telling me about her fifth boy friend, now her fiance. He was a young broker active in the New York Stock Market. From his picture I saw that he was a handsome and bright fellow.

"You are very lucky. I wish you happiness all your life," I said with heartfelt admiration.

"Thank you for your wishes and blessing." She

stopped combing her blond hair, turned to open a leather suitcase and took out an exquisite jewel case. From it she picked up a pair of gold earrings.

"Is this...beautiful?" she didn't know how to say gold earrings in Chinese.

"Gold earrings, beautiful, very beautiful."

She told me proudly that they were a gift her fiance gave her at San Francisco airport before she left for China. She said that when she arrived at Shanghai Railway Station, many Chinese were fascinated by the gold earrings, inlaid with black diamonds, swaying beneath her ears.

This was an outstanding and expensive pair of gold earrings, and also a symbol of love and happiness. But who would have thought that this pair of gold earrings would cause me a lot of trouble and nearly create an impassable chasm between us.

A Case of the Missing Gold Earrings

The incident occurred at the public lavatory on the third floor of the dormitory on March 29, our mutual birthday.

After lunch two short American girls were washing handkerchiefs and silk scarves in one corner and Ge Xinya and I were washing our hair in another.

Seeing her carefully take off the gold earrings, I said to her: "Take them back to the room." I meant to go on warning her that the dormitory, even for foreign students, was not safe and that things had been stolen before. But I did not want to slander our

Chinese character or make her feel unsafe, so I swallowed the words I was about to utter.

"It doesn't matter," she said and put the earrings beside her soap dish.

I closed my eyes and dipped my head, full of soap bubbles, into a basin of warm water.

Someone shouted, in a shrill, loud voice outside: "Ge Xinya, you are wanted on the phone! It's an international long distance call. Please come quickly!"

It was the voice of Wu Dewan, a student from Thailand whose family had recently moved to Colorado in the U.S.A. She was born in Bangkok and had a round face as cute as a doll. She lived on the second floor of the dormitory adjacent to the only telephone in the whole building.

I had finished washing my hair and returned to the room when Ge Xinya appeared at the door of our room, her eyes brimming with tears.

"Ge Xinya, who called you? What happened?"

"I am in trouble," she said sadly. "My fiance ... he ... he is sick."

"What's wrong with him," I asked anxiously.

"He said... he doesn't want to eat, or sleep, he is going crazy, perhaps something wrong with his nerves."

Oh well, I tried very hard to hold back my laughter. In the past I had heard that young people in Europe and America did not take their love affairs seriously. They changed their lovers like changing partners at a ball. I would not have expected that the young fellow could suffer from lovesickness and that she would shed so many tears.

To console my poor roommate, I teased her intentionally: "Don't worry, I can cure him."

She looked at me and asked sincerely: "How?"

"Buy an air ticket and fly back to his side. I'm sure he will fully recover at once."

"Ah," she suddenly woke up. "Mei Mei, how cunning you are!"

She smiled through tears and held me tightly around my neck with excitement. We both laughed and played for a good while, then she remembered that she had to finish washing her hair.

A few minutes later she rushed back to the room looking flustered. "Mei Mei, where are my gold earrings?" she asked anxiously.

"Didn't you take them with you when you went downstairs to answer the phone?" I asked her, without thinking.

"I forgot. I had no time for them at the moment. You were beside me then, you should have seen them," she said pointedly.

"But my head was covered with soap bubbles, how could I see?"

"If you didn't see them, who could?" Obviously she didn't quite believe me.

I am not the kind of person who is easily bullied. So I tried to defend myself and said: "After you left, I never set eyes on them again. And besides, you didn't tell me to watch them for you."

"Don't be angry, Mei Mei." Seeing my uncompromising stand, she changed and softened her tone a bit. "It's my fault because I didn't take care of my things and didn't tell you to do that for me when I left the lavatory in a hurry...."

I was feeling very uncomfortable at the moment and didn't hear the rest of what she said.

Just then the two short American girls arrived. They walked about three metres away from me and talked quickly in English. They thought I couldn't understand them, but actually I knew many of the words, such as "Chinese," "poor," "can't be trusted," so on and so forth.

I realized that the two short Americans were talking about me. Nothing could have been more humiliating.

Usually when things happen in China that do not turn out as we wish, we like to criticize our own country and admire Western civilization. However, at this moment when these Westerners were criticizing Chinese people in our own land without any reason, I was filled with indignation. I felt I should step forward and speak out to protect our national dignity.

I finally fired back with forceful words that flew from my mouth one after another as if I were shooting a machine gun.

"My dear ladies, you can suspect me and report the case to our Ministry of Public Security, or Interpol, or even to Mr. Sherlock Holmes. But, you should know that the ancient Chinese people expounded a profound philosophy of life, that is: 'a great man will never be misled by seduction of money and status and neither will he turn his coat because of his impoverished family and low social status.' You have no reason to draw an equal sign between poverty and untrustworthiness, let alone to link that with Chinese people! Otherwise you would find it hard to explain why you came to China from another continent to study."

The power of my forceful words and my vehement presentation seemed to have a strong influence. The two short Americans went silent and Ge Xinya's face flushed red. She walked beside me and tried to calm me down. "Mei Mei, don't ruin our friendship simply because of this trifling thing," she said making a gesture and shrugging her shoulders. "Let's forget about it."

"No, it is not over," I said solemnly. "Friendship is friendship and a case is a case. Let's go and report the case."

"To the Ministry of Public Security?"

"No, to the nearest local police station."

Delighted, But Bitter

A young man with a protruding stomach sat playing a fortune telling game in dead earnest at the office of the local police station.

"Sir, we came to report a case."

The man just sat there, playing his cards without lifting his eyelids. Perhaps he did not understand Ge Xinya's Chinese, so I said loudly after her: "I report a case. This American student lost her gold earrings."

Maybe my high voice shattered his good fortune as he suddenly gathered all the cards and put them on the table. He still kept silent.

"We have come to the wrong place, haven't we?" Ge Xinya asked timidly.

"This might be the deaf and dumb school," I replied ironically.

"Nonsense!" The man banged the table and finally rose to his feet, scattering the cards away.

Ge Xinya was frightened. She did not know what was happening, but kept saying: "I'm sorry to have bothered you." Seeing this I kept quiet.

For quite some time, none of us spoke a word. At last, the man opened the drawer and took out a book, "Registry of lost property."

"What's the name of the owner of the lost property?" he asked coldly.

"Ge Xinya."

"When was it lost?"

"Fifteen minutes ago."

"Where was it lost?"

"In the lavatory on the third floor of the small white building."

"Was there anyone around then?"

"Only me...."

"You?" he gave a snort of contempt.

His sneer and doubtful tone was like a chilling gust of cold wind and chilled me to the heart. What lousy luck! It was all right for foreigners to suspect me if they only talked behind my back. But who would have thought this man, a "dignified" officer of the local police station, could use freezing irony and burning satire to me in front of a foreigner. If this can be tolerated, what cannot?

"What's your name, please?"

"Wang Mei Mei."

"Which class, which grade and which department?"

"Class A, Grade 85 and Department of Chinese."

"Are you a Party member? A league member? A cadre? Have you received any honours or punishment?"

That was going too far. To my surprise, he started questioning me. His rudeness and arrogant tones could only scare a freshman away. For me, a junior student who had seen the world and experienced a lot of things in life in this famous university, however, it was powerless. Nothing could actually frighten me.

Well, stand still there, my friend. It's my turn now.

"I have a question, sir," I said lifting my head upward a little bit. "Am I the person who accompanied this American girl here to report the case or a prisoner you fetched for interrogation? If you want to interrogate me, please tell me first your name, age, birthplace, your background and personal historical records. What's more important is that you should also explain by which means you got this job that allows you to play cards in the office during work time and to rebuke people as you like?"

The man did not expect I could reply in such a brave way. His face flushed and turned pale by turns.

At this moment Ge Xinya forgot all her worries

of the lost gold earrings. She could not help murmuring: "Well done, Mei Mei. Your questions are wonderful and quite reasonable. This gentleman is very impolite and very cold no matter who he's talking to, a foreigner or a Chinese."

I felt much relieved, but at the same time I felt miserable because the person I had reprimanded was also a Chinese. If he had not assumed an arrogant and intimidating posture in front of me, his compatriot, I would not have responded that way to him before a foreigner.

On the way back to the dormitory Ge Xinya consoled me and kept saying: "Mei Mei, don't be upset. It will be cleared up some day."

Back at the dormitory, I still said nothing. I got on the bed, covered my head with sheet and wept.

I don't understand why people always like to suspect each other. I remained puzzled after pondering it a hundred times over; it was as if I had fallen into an abyss.

A World of Warmth and Cold

I don't know how long I slept. When I woke up, the room was very quiet. The hands of the clock pointed at eight. It was evening. I looked around and found under the lamp that my canteen was piled up with noodles and cabbages, with five-spiced oiled eggs on the top. Beneath the canteen was a little note on which was written clearly, in English:

"Mei Mei,

"If you feel lonely and depressed, please try to think that I will regard you as my faithful friend forever.

Ge Xinya"

I suddenly felt a warm current flow through my body and melt my frozen heart.

I walked out of my room and looked at my neighbours' rooms. They were all quiet and still. How strange! Where had the American girls gone?

Ah, in a flash I remembered it was my and Ge Xinya's birthday today. Didn't I settle it with her earlier that we would celebrate our birthday together in our room? But now she had gone with her friends. Did they want to avoid me — a Chinese girl they thought they could not trust? Well, Ge Xinya, you said one thing and meant another. You said that you would regard me as your faithful friend forever, but actually you acted differently. I finally saw through you.

My heart sank. I slowly tore the note to shreds and vowed to myself that once the truth of the case of missing gold earrings came out, I would move out of the small white building right away, returning to my former room 214, in Building One where it is crowded and noisy, but at least where I had peace of mind and didn't make friends with foreigners.

Thinking of this, I slammed the door and threw myself onto the bed. I felt isolated, abandoned, and became more depressed, lonely and indignant.

I didn't know the time when I heard a click at the door. The sound came from the lock. I quickly jumped out of bed. The door was opened wide. In front of me was a solemn, pious and inspiring scene. Accompanied by women's voices singing "Happy birthday to you," a cake as big as a pot lid, made to order, appeared. The 20 birthday candles were lit and Ge Xinya's cute round face shone red before the sparkling flames. Behind her followed our neighbours, more than ten American girls, and Wu Dewan, the girl from Thailand, was with them. Wu told me quietly that the American girls had already bought a cake from a department store for Ge Xinya and me. However, Ge Xinya suggested later that they should have a super large cake made for me, to comfort my wounded pride and make the atmosphere of the birthday celebration warmer and grander. She had firmly led the American girls to Guanshenyuan Bakery and Confectionery, a famous hundred-year-old shop. At that time the workers in the cake shop were about to leave for home. The American girls pleaded with them and Ge Xinya took out her own money for their overtime pay so the workers hastened to make a large fresh and delicate cake for me.

"I have a suggestion," Xia Weihua, one of the short American girls said loudly. "Let Mei Mei and Ge Xinya blow out the candles on the cake together, OK?"

All the people in the room agreed. Some were clapping their hands and some were shouting with excitement.

At this very moment, I could not see clearly, neither could I understand them completely. My eyes blurred and my heart was beating like waves lashing the shore.

"Mei Mei, what's the matter?" Ge Xinya embraced me and asked with deep emotion. "Have you seen my note: 'If you feel lonely and depressed, please try to think that I will regard you as my faithful friend forever.'?"

The note? I was suddenly startled. I had torn it into shreds. What should I say to her?

Oh, my friend, I know you are unhappy. Yes, who would not cry their heart out if a precious gift from a beloved one vanished suddenly? Even the richest princess would be deeply grieved and bitterly angry. But you, however, put aside your own sorrows temporarily, wrote the note to console me and ran around to have a cake made to cheer me up. It would be all right if all this happened at an ordinary time or after the thief were caught and the gold earrings returned to you in good condition, but that is not the case now. Someone still suspects me, is aware of me and looking down on me, while you respect and rely on me as usual and take better care of me. What you have done deeply moved me and made me want to cry on your shoulder.

I was too excited then to utter a single word. I took a deep breath and blew out all the birthday candles.

Before I finish this article, I have to make one thing clear. The lost gold earrings were finally found after several months by a plumber who came to repair the pipes. They were stuck at the neck of a drain pipe.

When Ge Xinya recovered her lost gold earrings, she drew me by the arm to the local police station. She said that she wanted to see the man again and make him rehabilitate my reputation. I walked a few steps with her and then stopped.

"Why don't you go?"

"Let's forget about it," I imitated her pronunciation saying it in Chinese.

Early this morning Ge Xinya showed me a telegram and told me that her boyfriend had arrived in Shanghai by plane yesterday evening and would come to Nanjing today by train. Now she can wear that pair of gold earrings and go to meet him at the railway station.

Americans and Divorce

Chen Fan

J IM told me: "Father has called from California and invited us to attend his wedding." How strange! Could it be that his parents had a son before they got married? But Jim was 32 years old. How could they have waited such a long time? So, I replied: "A son attends his father's wedding! This kind of joke is new for me." Jim frowned and, after a long pause, said dejectedly: "I am sorry. I wanted to hide this from you, my parents got divorced half a year ago and now Father is marrying another woman." My heart sank at this and I felt cold from head to foot.

I could hear all the gossip again, gossip aired when I was marrying Jim. "Good heavens! Married to a foreigner!... Americans are all bad.... Few of them stick to their first marriage.... Some day she will be abandoned by this American." At that time I really felt like explaining but what was the use? Deeply rooted in my countrymen are such established ideas as: to marry a foreigner is to betray China; divorce is immoral and so on and so forth. Americans, according to them, are hardened criminals of divorce. What is worse, Jim was really not a bachelor.

I almost didn't marry Jim because of his first

marriage. Though I had learned from his friend that it was his ex-wife who had divorced him, traditional Chinese ideas still drove me to grumble at him sometimes. When he couldn't bear it, he would fight back, "Why, do I have to criticize myself? I don't even know what I have done to be criticized about? Divorce is a painful thing, but not dirty. It's better to be realistic and separate in a friendly way than to live together without love. Of course, ending the marriage was not our desire. Who would not hope for a life full of love in his or her beloved's lifelong company? Many Americans do actually marry once and for all, but not everybody is so lucky. Love is never at a standstill; it depends on the joint efforts of husband and wife. It either grows and renews or withers away. In my opinion, quite a few Chinese couples have virtually separated, but they remain together for the sake of so-called virtue. Are they virtuous?"

I don't want our traditions to be defied by foreigners, but what Jim said had something in it. I know quite a few Chinese couples whose marriages have collapsed. Some have totally different characters and interests, some hold divergent views in politics and still some cannot balance their everyday lives. They all understand that the best solution is divorce but they don't take this last step due to all kinds of pressure from their children, relatives, work units and courts. I myself hold self-contradictory views on this matter. I loathe divorce, for it is miserable to break up a family. But I have every sympathy for those couples who want to divorce but cannot, because life is unbearable without love and hope. No matter whether you are Chinese or American, you always yearn for love and freedom. It is true that Chinese traditions advocate such virtue as "follow a chicken if you marry a chicken and follow a dog if you marry a dog." But what has been eulogized most is pure, spiritual love, as is manifested in such classic Chinese literature as *Song of Everlasting Remorse, Butterfly Lovers* and *A Dream of Red Mansions*. These widely loved Chinese classics praise not only those who "live to be under one roof and die to be within one cave," but also those who "can't live as husband and wife but will lie together after death." The difference is that the latter doesn't legalize their love. This shows that Chinese traditions encourage people to search for real love. However, the fact that real love in these classics always ends in tragedy indicates that something in our traditions smothers humanity.

After more than one year in the United States I found that the overwhelming majority of the people were energetic. I attributed this to the stimulation of money, but even more so to love, although that love can be deep or shallow, spiritual or sexual. Everyone seeks to be loved and also to love. This is human nature. Among my acquaintances some are bathed in love, some are searching and some waiting. Tomorrow is another day and a new hope for them. This is the motive force of society. Free is their affection, no matter whether you appreciate them or despise them. They live a happier and more relaxed life than those loveless and hopeless

Chinese couples.

Nevertheless, reason cannot always sway emotions. When Jim told me his parents were separated and his father was remarrying, I admit to feeling somewhat disgusted. I thought it must be his father who was to blame; he must be fickle in affection. But, to my surprise, Jim said: "As a matter of fact, Father has no other alternative. In past years, Mother and he didn't get along well."

"Then, why did they get married if they were incompatible?" I asked.

"They were passionately in love for a period of time. Since it was a second marriage for Mother, my paternal grandfather was firmly opposed to it, but Father was resolved. Later, their differences developed. Father was a sports fan and not good at words; while Mother loved the arts and conversation and later even became a nit-picker. When together, they seldom felt happy. I always feared that they would get divorced but that may have been the only way both of them could get a change for the better." Tears filled his eyes.

Cases like this are not rare in China. One need only think of those marriages made during the "cultural revolution" when students went to the countryside for re-education. For many couples, crimson dreams of love were soon replaced by the black-and-white reality of marriage. Could I ask these unfortunate people "why did you get married?" I remember several years ago when I went to a far-away mountain area to visit a young intellectual who had remained there after the campaign to go to the countryside. The scene upon entering his house stunned me. His wife and two children were playing cards and shouting while this labour-hardened scholar was in a corner preparing his lessons. He said, "In the sky, we'd be a pair of lovebirds; and on earth, we'd be couple of interlocking branches." I learned afterwards that he had a girlfriend before coming to the countryside who later deserted him because of his family's unclear political record. During his term of hard labour this country girl had given him sympathy and help and they got married and had two children. He once got an opportunity to divorce his wife and resume urban life but conscience stopped him. He would not betray the tradition that one should not forget his poor and lowly friends or abandon his wife who shared his hard lot, though he often regretted this and suffered from their incompatibility. I admired his moral character but regret his unhappy marriage. He lost too much. Divorce is cruel, but the binds of a lovelesss marriage are inhuman. Isn't there any other way out?

Then I think of my aging parents. One of them is involved with literature and the other teaches physical culture. Their characters and habits are anything but the same, but Chinese conventions have tied them together, even through the "cultural revolution." When I asked my mother what had kept them together, she said that it was not love, but the proverb "content is happiness." This is the remedy the older generation always prescribes for young people. What a pity that this prescription is not all-powerful, especially for people seeking love.

Once the idea of divorce occurs to a couple, their marriage is like a terminal illness. What right did I have to blame Jim's parents? Marriage was their own affair and they surely had no obligation to inherit Chinese traditions. But still, Jim and I will not attend the wedding because we do not want to. To comfort his mother, we invited her to come and stay with us for a few days. To my surprise, she was still enthusiastic and did not look sad. And what is more, she had signed up to be a student of Jim's father and learn racquetball from him after class. I really cannot understand these Americans! How could they get divorced and still be on good terms? Including Jim, they seem to have no enmity towards their former spouses and can help each other when necessay. I guess that Americans' feelings are not as deep and strong as those of the Chinese. In China, where there is so much love there should also be much hatred. But Jim said: "You're too arbitrary to reach this conclusion. It is easy for Americans to go through the procedures for divorce, but deep in their hearts they are greatly hurt. I cried for quite a few days over my divorce but my common sense won. Love is not to possess. It is selfish and stupid to hate your beloved if you can't get her or him. If we cannot go together, then let's each go our own way. Love does not deteriorate, but is left in the past forever. You think Mother is not grieved? She still loves Father deeply, only she does not want to show that. I feel that after divorce she became more serious. She has taken up a teaching post to enrich her single life and free herself from household affairs. In this sense, divorce is not a bad thing for her. But she often feels lonely, and this is bad."

That evening, we had dinner in a Chinese restaurant. To our dismay, Jim's mother unfolded a note placed in the fortune cookie which read: "He has done his best to love you but still he does not love you with all his heart." We were struck dumb, but Mother, seeming not to care, put it into her pocket and said: "It must be God's will to let me take this note home to show my daughters." She tried to appear calm, but I could see tears well up in her eyes. "Poor Mom, if only she could marry again." I thought. Only those who have lost their treasure know how to take care of it. I hope that people will learn to safeguard their treasure before they lose it.

I thought that Jim's sisters would dislike their father's new wife. Contrary to my expectations, they all attended the wedding and even wrote us to say they liked the new wife. Before long, Father and his new wife flew specially to see us. At the airport, we were pleased to see a completely new Father: healthy and vigorous. He looked at least 10 years younger than last year when he was old, depressed and listless. His new wife, Betty, was a gymnastics teacher even though she was older than 50. Graceful and well dressed, she was very cordial and soon became a good friend. In less than 10 days she won praise from relatives and neighbours with her erudition and versatility, and with her amicability, diligence and understanding. At a party, watching Father and Betty enjoying themselves dancing, Jim said with emotion: "I haven't seen Father so happy since I was born and I am really glad. Betty is very well suited to him. My resentment towards her has disappeared.

Before departure, Betty told me that she had never loved anyone as she loved Jim's father, who was far more considerate and attentive than her deceased husband. I was moved by her happiness. I realized there had originally been three unfortunate persons, but now at least two had obtained happiness—and perhaps Jim's mother will get her share of love some day. The world lost one couple but gained a pair of lovers. The children still have their mother and father, plus one more relative. This outcome of a divorce is not necessarily ugly and tragic. Of course, I still dare not and will not appreciate divorce, but I will not simply curse it. For I know it is the last resort of unhappy people.

On the way back from the airport, I thought of my own marriage, of Jim's love for me and my own future. If some day I should leave Jim, I will face it philosophically. I believe that love will never wither away if we constantly try to perfect ourselves. Throughout my life, I will pray for love and wish that all lovers become husband and wife and that all husbands and wives will be deeply in love with each other.

A Greedy Landlord

Qian Yi

IN the U.S., universities only supply a limited number of dormitories for students. Most students have to rent rooms, so around universities there are landlords. The first headache for students and visiting scholars from China is to find a room after they have arrived in the country. Their experiences and luck differ but I know that I suffered a great deal from a greedy American landlord.

I arrived in July and one of my friends found me the room of an American student who had gone home for his summer vacation. Because I was warned that I would have to move out in the middle of August, I immediately began to look for a room with the help of friends. I copied down a long list of addresses and telephone numbers from the ads in local newspapers and bulletins posted by the Family Housing Section of the university. Then I telephoned and arranged to see the houses. As some houses were too far away from the university, some had no furniture, some required high rents and some landlords didn't allow me to use their kitchens, my long list was soon cut short. I had begun to worry when my friend Lily invited me to visit a Mr. Lower.

As soon as we entered Mr. Lower's office, we noticed a large board on the wall filled with small, closely written addresses. Keys were hanging under at least ten of them. We couldn't help exchanging a look of pleasant surprise: "We've found a landlord with so many houses that there must be a suitable one for us."

Mr. Lower, talking with two American students at the time, had silvery hair and a glowing face. He was not tall and was a little bit fat. He motioned us to sit down and wait. In a moment he asked us to go over. When he understood our purpose, he said: "I've got a two-bedroom flat with a kitchen and a bathroom and quiet, beautiful surroundings. It's good for you two Chinese women to stay in as companions." He even offered to drive us to have a look at the house.

On the way, he chatted with us, showing an interest in China and expressing his hope to tour China some day and his concern with whether we were getting used to our new life in America. All this left a good impression and led me to believe he was a kind old man. The house was satisfactory, particularly as it was near the university and not far from the supermarket. After consulting each other, Lily and I made an appointment with Mr. Lower to sign a contract the next day. One American student was still living in the house when we examined it but Mr. Lower told us he would soon move out.

Unexpectedly, the same Mr. Lower treated us quite differently the next day. To start with, he asked for such a high rent that it gave me a scare. Fortunately we were well informed about renting houses, so we rejected his price and bargained heatedly before reaching an agreement. Then he turned to the cash deposit. He wanted us to pay one month's rent as a deposit plus both the first and last month's rent. Such an amount not only exceeded our allowance, but also did not conform to accepted practices. We argued with him but he stuck to his demands. Considering the difficulty in finding a house, we had no alternative but to surrender. He even asked us to pay the money within three days of signing the contract. We suggested we pay on the day we moved in but he refused. The marathon talks lasted more than two hours until we were exhausted. We were fully aware that what he was really after was the bank interest for the intervening half month. Walking outside, Lily smiled: "This old man is too astute, we've fallen into his trap." What she didn't realize was that the worst was yet to come.

We asked Mr. Lower for the key one day before we intended to move in and he gave it to us without a word. We went excitedly to the new house intending to look it over. No sooner did we open the door than the American student came towards us, astonished that we entered without knocking. We explained we were the new tenants and were going to move in the next day. These words amazed him. He told us his lease didn't expire until August 20 and he wouldn't leave until then. Now it was our turn to be surprised. We read the two contracts; his expired on August 20, ours was valid from August 16. Both leases had Mr. Lower's signature. What was this all about? Was Mr. Lower just too old and forgetful?

Full of suspicion we went to Mr. Lower's. He assumed an innocent air and said casually, "What? Hadn't he moved out? I guessed that he had already left. What shall I do if he hasn't? Maybe it's better for you yourselves to talk with him." It was obvious that he knew everything. He had deceived us for the five days' rent. He had also left us without a room. Indignantly, we insisted that he solve the problem. He tried both hard and soft tactics on us and after an hour's battle of words, he promised to provide temporary rooms.

The next day we moved into the two temporary rooms, which were in the same building. Lily's room was on the second floor, while mine was just a basement. We felt a bit relieved because we finally had somewhere to stay but it soon became apparent we were again caught in Mr. Lower's trap. Lily first discovered that though there was a kitchen and a bathroom attached to her room, the water pipes hadn't been connected. She could not cook, bathe or even wash her face, needless to say use the toilet. Just as she went downstairs to tell me her discovery, I found my room had no electricity. I couldn't turn on the light. The room was shrouded in darkness before the sun set. How could I sleep by myself in this kind of room, let alone study? We telephoned Mr. Lower at his office and home but he was away for the weekend. We ate some food listlessly and went to Lily's room. We had to accompany each other to my basement at night if we wanted to use the toilet. Thus we spent two days and three nights. On Monday we informed Mr. Lower of all this but again he didn't show any sign of concern: "We haven't finished repairing the house. My workers are still on vacation." He neither took steps to solve our problems nor gave us an apology. We only got several candles and a box of matches. We could bear him no longer, yet what could we do? He had already taken away three months' rent and a lawsuit could end up costing even more money, especially as we were unfamiliar with American law. The only thing we could do was argue with him that his rooms were below the minimum housing standard and demand the return of five days' rent. To Mr. Lower, taking money out of his pocket was like cutting off a piece of his flesh. He haggled with us for hours before eventually consenting to return three days' rent as compensation.

The ten months spent in his house were not calm and peaceful. We had several more disputes with him over the fact that the refrigerator and radiator didn't work. When the lease was going to expire, Mr. Lower came to see us once on his own initiative. He praised us and was all smiles: "You Chinese women are the most peaceful ones. You pay more attention to sanitation and hygiene than others. I like such tenants like you the best." He then volunteered to install a new refrigerator, new curtains and so on. When he saw we were not moved and persisted in leaving, he went away in a huff.

Being sure that he might make trouble to hinder us, we gave the rooms a thorough cleaning before we left. As Mr. Lower couldn't find any fault with us while examining the rooms, he criticized us for using the wrong type of detergent to clean the kitchen and subtracted $20 from our cash deposit. He had really gone too far but we didn't feel like quarrelling with him any more.

In our opinion, he was so greedy that he seemed both detestable and funny. He made nearly a million dollars a year from his hundreds of houses, but he still racked his brains and took great pains to gain $10 or $20. Wasn't he pitiful?

Good-bye, Mr. Lower, you greedy American landlord.

The Judy I Know

Min Dahong

JUDY Polumbaum flew to Beijing on September 17, 1987 from San Franscisco. As a visiting scholar invited by the Research Institute of Journalism of the Academy of Social Sciences of China, Judy would stay in China for one year to study China's news media and to collect material for her doctoral thesis. I was asked to receive her at Capital Airport in Beijing on behalf of the institute that evening.

It was not difficult to spot her with her two children despite the crowds. However, not having seen her for a few years, I was surprised to see how slender she had become. Her four-year-old son was tugging her clothes, looking around curiously and timidly. The younger one was only nine months old. He sat in a baby carriage, sucking from a bottle.

Thus, on her trip to China, Judy had fulfilled her desire to take her two sons to her husband's home country.

Judy was born in Boston in 1953. Her father, Teddy, was a noted American photographer who had applauded the founding of the People's Republic of China in 1949. In the McCarthy Era, however,

Teddy suffered persecution for his political views. Perhaps for that very reason Judy became interested in China. She studied Chinese history and culture in university, even learning to write Chinese characters. Now she can read, write and speak Chinese very well.

Judy came to China for the first time in 1975 when China was still undergoing the "cultural revolution." She came with a group of college students as guests of the Chinese People's Association for Friendship with Foreign Countries. During that visit, she worked at the Shanghai Electrical Machinery Plant and with peasants in Dazhai. She also discussed Zhang Chunqiao's newly published article "On Overall Dictatorship over Capitalist Class" with her friends. Though she was deeply impressed by the Chinese people's hard work and perseverance, she could not understand what was meant by "limiting the right of the capitalist class." After all, three weeks is too short a time to understand a foreign country. Since then, however, she had looked forward to knowing China more profoundly and thoroughly.

In 1979, Judy came to work as an expert both at *China Daily* and in the Foreign News Department of Xinhua News Agency. Meanwhile she also taught English news reporting and editing in the Department of Journalism at the Academy of Social Sciences of China (ASSC). This was when the Communist Party of China was trying to bring order out of chaos after the Third Plenary Session of its Eleventh Central Committee. China took its first steps in economic reform and opening to the outside world. The news media was trying to break the shackles locked on it by Lin Biao and the "gang of four." But old habits die hard. Outdated modes of thinking, stereotyped writing and dull and dry language still prevailed in news reports. During this stay in China, which lasted until 1982, Judy was no longer simply an onlooker. She devoted all her efforts to helping improve China's news media and to train qualified journalists.

Both the Research Institute of Journalism and the graduate college of the ASSC were founded in 1978. The 70-odd postgraduates enrolled in the first year lived in Building 15 of the People's Daily. When Judy came to teach them in 1979, I was studying the history of China's newspapers and journals and had no direct contact with her. One day, however, word spread among the students that Judy had made a declaration in class: "I will get a Chinese husband for myself." Before long she had won the heart of Gao Yuan, a student in her class from Shijiazhuang, Hebei Province. They got married in Beijing in 1980 and both went to the United States in 1982.

Their life in America was not easy. Though Judy taught at Standford University, she had to study hard for her doctorate. Gao studied economic management for an MBA. After graduation in the summer of 1988 he got a temporary job. In addition to that, their sons Taihang and Tianjiao were born. So for several years, they were quite hard up.

Judy's family life, however, is happy and rich.

She said approvingly of Gao when asked what had become of him recently: "Many of the Chinese youths coming to study in America are money oriented. Gao is not that kind. He only knows how to study hard. He does not care much about what he wears, either. He will wear anything I buy for him. I'm especially pleased with that." From Judy I also know her husband does not have American citizenship, although he has been there for several years. "Of course, nor do I become a Chinese citizen merely because I am the daughter-in-law of a Chinese family," she said. It seems both Judy and Gao Yuan have retained some sort of personal independence. Their sons are lovely. Taihang looks more Chinese than Tianjiao. When he goes out with his mother people look at him up and down and ask if he is Chinese. Judy expresses her affection towards China by saying: "My heart, just like my family, is half American and half Chinese."

During her stay in China this time, besides her own research work, Judy also took up teaching in the Foreign Languages Department of Beijing Broadcasting Institute. In May 1988, she was invited to Guangzhou for two weeks to give classes and lectures at Jinan University. As is well-known today, it is not easy to attract college students to a class in which faults will be criticised. But Judy's teaching was more than a success.

Judy taught students how to do interviews and write news reports. Every lesson was interesting and was welcomed by the students. Today, when Chinese education faces a crisis, the popular belief that "learning is of no use" is prevalent from primary schools all the way to graduate schools. Outdated teaching contents and methods have made students bored with school. Judy's teaching, however, has widened our approach. The method of "containing teaching in pleasure" endorsed by ancient Chinese educators has been used very flexibly by this Westerner.

Judy smiles to everyone she meets, a sincere smile, a smile of good intentions. Everyone she meets is affected by that smile.

One day, Judy showed me photos she had taken of the graduate class of the Foreign Languages Department of Beijing Broadcasting Institute. She remarked: "From photos you can tell the differences between students when you graduated and those in the 80's. In the photos of your grade, you look all very serious." After carefully examining the new photos, I had to admit this. The girls were beautifully dressed while boys either stretched their arms or held up two fingers into a "V." Judy and all the others in the photos were full of smiles. Those students are dear to her heart.

When Judy decided to take her two sons with her to China almost all her relatives and friends thought she was crazy. They urged her to change her mind, saying the trip would separate her from not only her husband, but also the convenient living conditions to which she was accustomed. It is hard to imagine how one can do research and teaching while fulfilling a mother's role in entirely new surroundings. Yet Judy has succeeded in doing all this.

Perhaps the Chinese know better how difficult it is for her — people who know her say Judy is really *liaobuqi* (great). Once Judy said frankly: "Life is really too tense for me. I don't even know what freedom is."

During her stay in Beijing, Judy lived at the Beijing Broadcasting Institute in the eastern suburbs, quite far from the centre of the city. She bought a bicycle a few days after her arrival. When she went to the city, she would have to spend two hours coming and going by bicycle or take the over-crowded buses just like a Beijing citizen.

Once Judy wrote an interesting article on Beijing's buses and traffic, "Love and Hate for the Streets," which was carried in *Beijing Daily* on June 28, 1988. It described taking buses as a life and death fight for people. She also wrote of the kind-hearted souls who gave her a helping hand. Under her pen, "Beijing is not a city to make you feel lethargic. It can make you love it madly. It can also make you hate it to extremes."

Judy can be called a good wife and mother even by Chinese standards. Every time her mother-in-law came to see her, Judy would go to the railway station to receive her. When the mother-in-law left, she would see her off at the station. Once when the elderly woman wanted to buy a curtain for her new house, Judy rode to a shop in Qianmen in snowy weather.

Judy doesn't spoil her children though she loves them dearly. She does not think their every wish should be satisfied. Both Taihang and Tianjiao were sent to the kindergarten of the institute. Taihang likes to be dressed in an army uniform and to play with toy guns. He is extremely fond of the TV series *Journey to the West* and the cartoon *Black Cat the Inspector*. Tianjiao is making fast progress in listening to and speaking Chinese in the kindergarten. Judy was very happy to see the progress the children were making. So she wrote "My Two Kids Are Living Happily in China" for *China Daily* (May 9, 1988). Radio Beijng asked her to do a recording of the article for broadcast.

Judy does not care much for material life. She dresses plainly and always invited me to stay for a meal when I visited her home. "We'll just have instant noodles," she would say.

She shows a strong enthusiasm for work. In February 1988 Shanghai was plagued by hepatitis A, so I suggested she postpone a planned business trip. "Doesn't matter," she said. "I'll be there just for one day. I'll not eat for the whole day." She did not change her mind until I warned her of the possibility that her children might be affected which, in turn, could hurt the whole kindergarten.

Judy is also an activist for Sino-American friendship. She never refuses to do anything for that cause. When the Beijing Office of the Ford Fundation held its opening ceremony, she was a busy photographer. When the grand Symposium on Sino-American Industrial, Trade and Economic Development was held in June 1988 in Beijing, she was the drafter of the 20 one-minute toasts. She was more than once called a "China hand," but she always said very modestly that her understanding of Chinese affairs was still very superficial. She thought reform had given hope to China. As to the achievements of the reforms, she made a very good comparison: China is now like a bottle which is half filled with water. One can say it is half empty, yet one can also say it is at least half full.

Time passed swiftly. On July 15, 1988 Judy would fly back to America. She told me, "The nearer it is to my day of departure, the more my affection to China becomes."

Yes, half of Judy's heart is in China. I expect, and those in the field of journalism in China expect, Judy will again fly to China from the "other side of the large river."

Americans Around Me

Jiao Xing

Through Customs

EVERYTHING was novel to Xiao K when he went abroad for the first time.

He had seen America, with its advanced science and technology, only on TV. Now he was very excited because he would see skyscrapers and other modern things with his own eyes. Simultaneously, he felt a little bit proud of himself. Think of this, in such a big country as China those who have got through TOEFL (Test of English as a Foreign Language) and GRE (Graduate Record Examination) and have been admitted as graduate students by a famous American university can really be counted as rare. For his flight to America his relatives had emptied their pockets to help him. How could he take it with ease? In addition, the land he was going to was unknown to him, so was his future. He closed his eyes and pondered his triumph, then reminded himself not to let his imagination run wild.

"What do you want to drink?" A soft voice startled Xiao K.

It was a hostess who came to offer drinks. Xiao K glanced sideways at the varied bottles and cans over the trolley.

With his shoulders squared, he answered bravely: "Orange juice."

Actually what he really wanted to drink was Coca Cola, which was frequently shown on TV advertisements. But the only words he was sure he could say perfectly right were orange juice. Furthermore, he had more sensed the hostess' question than actually understand it. Why is the English spoken by foreigners is so different from that by Chinese?

The plane landed safely in F city. Now Xiao K would step out in America. Passengers were going out of the compartment in order, while the crew stood at the doorway saying "thank you" and "good-bye" to the passengers. How ridiculous! During a flight of over a dozen hours they had served drinks and meals and cared for the passengers with deep concern. It was they who should have been thanked. (Attendants on trains in China suddenly appeared in Xiao K's mind: Their faces were always long as if passengers owed them debts.) Then Xiao K realized that United Airlines was a privately run company, so bad manners would mean fewer passengers, fewer passengers would mean less business and less business could mean cuts in staff.

At the luggage claim centre, lights glistened even though it was day time. Wasn't it a waste to turn on all those lamps? The hall was rather crowded. The people shuttling back and forth in front of him were all fair and blue-eyed. Most women, both young and old, wore make-up and were fashionably dressed, ornaments clattering and high heels clicking. They smelled of strange perfumes when they passed by. Some men were dressed up in jackets and ties but many others wore informal clothes like blue jeans. It seemed to Xiao K there were also a few black-haired people in this hall, but he was not sure whether they were Chinese. At this moment he felt terribly lonely and longed to speak with somebody. He was a bit dizzy. Perhaps the effect of the perfume? Or the eye-dazzling light? He stepped aside and stood by the No. 4 luggage conveyer. The belt rolled on in silence, carrying out passengers' luggage, which they picked up with no hubhub, no pushing and shoving. Armed policemen were patrolling here and there, with walkie-talkies and batons in their hands.

Xiao K felt a little bit sick from the mixture of perfume and the smell wafting from the buffet.

He was being examined at customs, where a lady served him quite amiably. With her thin and pale hands, she turned the pages of his passport quickly. "Ah, her red nails are nearly one *cun* (3.33 cm)!" As he was wondering, she asked him a series of questions. She spoke so quickly, so softly and with so many words together. Xiao K was sweating, and at a complete loss as to what to say. (It was spring but he was wearing two sweaters, two woollen undershirts, a western-style suit and an overcoat. No wonder he was sweating.) Finally he was released by her "OK."

He left with her hands and ten long red nails still swaying before his eyes. "My goodness! How can she manage to cook at home? Her nails are too long."

New House

Xiao K let himself relax after he hung up the last of his clothes. "At last, I've managed to settle down."

His room, at least 18 to 19 square metres, was tidy and clean, and smelled of detergent. Seeing the expensive bedcover and rough woollen blanket, he suddenly felt completely exhausted, as if all the fatigue of his trip had assailed him at once. He lay down and closed his eyes but could not fall asleep. Perhaps he was too excited.

It was a rather worn-out white house, with lush green trees and a lawn around it. But plants and grass were only roughly trimmed. The interior maintenance of the house seemed coarse and crude. The four big bedrooms, the toilet, the kitchen and the corridor, which were all white-washed, told Xiao K that the house had been designed originally for a family. Three tenants had already rented the other rooms, so he was in the fourth one. Three men and one woman shared the kitchen and toilet. Would it be convenient? He had not imagined there would also be such a "compound" with mixed residents in the States! He could not help laughing.

It was very beautiful early the next morning. Sunlight gushed out of the azure sky through colourful clouds, then danced over the lawn through

the dense woods. Xiao K was standing at the door
of the house, gazing into the empty street. Occasionally a car broke the silence and sped by. The morning, though, did not seem to belong to him. He felt
sad and sighed to himself, "I am part of the other
world. It's really 'a broken heart at the ends of the
earth'." Only a few days had passed since he had left
his home and he was already homesick. Why were
no people walking in the streets? It was so different
from home.

*... The morning bell had just tolled five times and
mist still clogged the air. All the streets and alleys were
already bustling with excitement.*

*The sound of bicycle bells accompanied the stream
of people going to work. Vegetable peddlers were
carrying wheel barrows and crying "Vegetables selling cheap, fresh cucumber, green cabbages." They
tried to sell as much as possible on their way to
markets. Pupils would leave their homes later, and
now must be having their breakfast. Housewives with
baskets were going to markets, chatting about food:
"Fish prices will be raised again today. More and
more eggs can be seen these days." Or just gossiping:
"The Zhang family arranged 20 tables of drinks and
dishes at their son's wedding feast." They always took
keen pleasure in spreading rumours. And Xiao K
realized from their behaviour why there is the saying
"A sesame can be exaggerated into a watermelon."*

*There were also girls in the streets, in T-shirts, blue
jeans and long hair, to which Xiao K was not used.
Once he saw a girl swaggering around in a T-shirt
with the English words "Nude Girl" printed on it. He*

was very upset.

All this had passed and never belonged to this new world. "Now, I'm here." Xiao K drew his thoughts back to reality.

An unknown "colleague" (who was labelled as "colleague" only because he was Chinese) volunteered to be his guide to look for an apartment, at the same time acting as his interpreter. They had been to several places, but here prices were too high, and there cooking was forbidden. The colleague complained all the time, "Well, what if you had a car. Then we would not have to look for a room around the university." At first Xiao K did not understand what he meant and then he thought better of it. It is true that houses around the university were "daughters of an emperor, without a worry about being married off." But why not allow him to cook? Maybe the Americans only eat raw vegetables? The colleague then answered vaguely that Americans did actually seem just to eat raw vegetables.

At last they pressed the door bell of a small house with great hope. First came the barking of a dog, then a fit of rustling, and then the door was opened by a tall but fat old lady who stood there in bare feet. She was wearing a cotton print dress without a waistline and a pair of glasses. Her gray hair was in disorder and perspiration spread over her forehead.

"Hi, sweety, come in please," she greeted them smiling. Xiao K's colleague had phoned her beforehand so she knew about their visit. As for why she called them "sweety" at first sight, Xiao K did not know since he had never heard any explanation about it when he had been learning English at home. His colleague sat down on the arm of a sofa and began to talk with the old woman, while Xiao K hesitated over which seat to take. All the seats were already occupied by seven or eight cats, and one black dog was sitting on the rug, on guard against the two guests. He probably would have attacked them if the old lady had not grabbed his leather collar. The dog was "glaring like a tiger eyeing its prey." Xiao K felt embarrassed. The room could be described as a mess. Papers were spread all over the desk as well as ink bottles, pens, needles and thread and a half-done woollen sweater. The old woman turned all the drawers out to the floor and rummaged through the muddle for the contract form. Xiao K may have known that among "the 36 stratagems, the best is running away," but his colleague winked at him persistently and whispered that the old woman was famous for her kindness and honesty. "It's not bad to be her tenant." At last the negotiations were finished. The colleague told Xiao K that if he was not satisfied with the room they could look elsewhere.

Xiao K vaguely heard the old woman introducing herself as Debi Smallack. Mrs. Smallack (her husband's family name) did not stop talking until they went out of her small room. Xiao K could understand only part of what she said but he sensed she was telling them that both her house and her furniture were in good order.

She did not lie. Xiao K fell in love with the room as soon as he entered it. Everything was perfect — the snow white walls, the white bookshelf, the clean desk, the milky white lamp, the pair of sofas, the small side-table, the almost new single bed along the wall, and the built-in wardrobe. The violet carpet, the hardwood floor and the air conditioner were to Xiao K's satisfaction. He was especially taken by the big oil painting on the main wall, which showed that the hostess' taste was not bad. Only a few persons in China could have afforded to install an air conditioner at home. (Perhaps in China cadres higher than a certain level are entitled to such treatment? Xiao K remembered he had not seen this thing at his school president's house. Thinking that his standard of living was now even higher than the president's he felt immensely proud.)

The bargain was struck and a half-year lease signed. It was decided that Xiao K would pay $140 per month, with $150 as a cash deposit. Xiao K carried his two cases, one big and one small, and a travelling bag full of books into his room.

What remained strange to him was why Mrs. Smallack lived in such a miserable room. She was not so poor.

Housemates

Cooking turned out to be a big problem for Xiao K, who had never paid attention to such a thing at home. Now nobody was using the kitchen so he seized this opportunity to practise his cooking skills.

But just after he had lit up the gas cooker, a gust of perfume, irritating to his nose, floated into the kitchen.

"Hi, are you the newcomer?" A gaudily made up woman appeared behind him. Xiao K had goosebumps all over because of the shock and the heavy foreign perfume, to which he was still not accustomed to. Her artificially painted face — she should have applied more powder to her neck, which was now a different colour than her whitewashed face — and the pair of huge golden earrings touching her shoulders were ridiculous in his eyes. She wore a pink, rose-patterned T-shirt with a plunging neckline, and tight black silk trousers. The trousers were also glistening. When Xiao K widened his eyes out of curiosity he saw there were countless golden buttons on them from the outer thigh to the waist. With every step she took Xiao K feared her plump lower body would break out of the tightly wrapped trousers. Her feet were in a pair of embroidered high-heeled slippers, again glistening. Her sexy, blood-red lips were always in an "O" shape every time she opened her mouth to speak, and her eyes and eyebrows also danced expressively. Xiao K was flustered — should he look straight at her or avoid her eyes?

Fortunately, the woman did not expect any answer. All she wanted was a listener. She talked and talked on without noticing whether Xiao K liked to hear. Half an hour later he knew not only her own story but also some things about their landlady. Miss Z said she herself came from Southeast Asia but was an ethnic Chinese and so could speak Chinese. Her purpose in coming to F city was to seek a husband. She was so rich that she could live here as long as she wished, and she did not need to worry about her studies. However, she had failed to find a becoming man for the whole year and a half. In a word, gentlemen at the Univeristy of F were too short-sighted and did not realize that she would be a beautiful wife. Hearing this sort of talk, Xiao K flushed and turned pale by turns because he had never heard any woman speaking so frankly to him. He guessed that this must be one of the aspects of "Western culture." Not until now had Xiao K understood the real meaning of cultural shock.

Xiao K plucked up his courage and said: "Miss Z, I am sorry, I am cooking."

Miss Z was immersed in her chatting and answered carelessly: "All right, cook more and invite me to have this dinner with you, OK?" She seated herself at the table and shifted the topic to their hostess.

"How much rent do you pay?" Miss Z asked with great interest.

"One hundred and forty dollars."

"Oh, price raised again. You know? The Yankee who had lived in your room before paid only $130 a month. This old woman is good at making money. She always raises the rent $10 each time she has a new tenant," Miss Z said angrily.

"Do you know how cheap this old woman is? Her refrigerator is a used one, so is her air conditioner. Four people share two refrigerators — how could that be sufficient? I buy food every week worth at least $200." Miss Z was complaining and trimming her pretty long red nails with a small file at the same time.

Xiao K gave out a vague "oh" sound and kept on cooking. Now he realized why his food had to be put in the lowest and smallest box of the refrigerator. Even so, he could not fill it. But in the middle there was a box full of chocolate, cream cookies and various canned foods.

"This old woman is terribly cunning and she would evade responsibility with tricks. Once the kitchen drain was blocked but she did not come to repair and clean the kitchen until she had got ten several phone calls. We paid our rent in vain." Miss Z was growing excited.

"Where is her husband?" Xiao K could not help interrupting.

"Never mention him. It serves her right to be so unfortunate. Didn't you see a madman playing with water outside? That's her husband. Ten years ago he was a famous professor, always charming in coat and tie. But his brain was destroyed in a car accident, and then he went mad. A vegetable! Sometimes I feel very frightened when I come back at night," Miss Z said. (She spoke a mixture of English and Chinese. It was obvious she was proud of her ability to convey her feelings, especially in front of a newly arrived Chinese.)

So the deranged old man he had seen beating water on the road with a stick while Mrs. Smallack cleaned grass away from her house was her husband!

What Miss Z said presented a vivid picture in Xiao K's mind: Mrs. Smallack had to carry the heavy burden of family life after her husband's accident. She repaired her own rooms and rented them but lived with her husband in the garage, which had been converted into an extra room. She had to take care of her mad husband and her rented house at the same time. They lived on the earnings from the house. She maintained electrical equipment, weeded the lawn, cleaned the house and so on. She had to do everything herself. Although Miss Z talked about her with scorn, Xiao K thought she was very brave.

And it turned out that Mrs. Smallack really was a kind-hearted, hard-working and honest woman. When Xiao K gave her a package of Chinese tea to express his respect for her, she was too happy to respond. When she heard that Xiao K's comprehension of spoken English was still not good, she got a tape recorder from her room for him to learn English, counting it as a piece of rented furniture and refusing to receive any money for it. In addition, she returned his $150 cash deposit when his lease expired. Over the next three years Xiao K moved several times and never got his full deposit back, different landlords using various excuses to deduct from it.

Several days later, Xiao K came back from jogging, sweating all over. At the door of the bathroom he met two gentlemen he was very familiar with — Miss Z's information certainly. One of them was tall and strong, with disordered blond hair reaching his shoulders. He was shirtless, a towel on his shoulder. The other one was somewhat fat, his eyes were always smiling and his short brown hair stood erect like a hard brush. He was also stripped to the waist, wearing a pair of white shorts.

"Hi, guy! Are you Chinese? Chinese are nice. My name is Jack, he is Jim Fatty."

"Hi, Mr. Fatty!" Xiao K politely greeted Jim, prompting a burst of laughter from the pair. Xiao K felt the blood rushing to his face but did not realize what mistake he had made.

"Never mind, he was kidding. My name is Jim Johnson," Jim explained.

Xiao K smiled awkwardly. From then on, he became more cautious and never ventured to call a strange man Mr. So-and-So. Who knows how many Americans there were that loved kidding at first sight? (Xiao K again could not help making a comparison between the characteristics of Chinese and Westerners. Chinese are generally inward looking, cautious and timid, so they would keep a distance from each other on first meeting and introduce themselves politely. The Westerners are more extroverted and open on first meeting, but he was not sure what a true friend looked like.)

Xiao K noticed that Jack and Jim very seldom cooked. He was confused why they ate raw celery and hot pepper, let alone cucumber and tomato. The boxes that belonged to them in the refrigerator were the least full, usually holding only butter, cheeze and milk. Every time they came back from outside the first thing they did was drink a big glass of milk, as if they were drinking water. (Who knows how they digested it? Xiao K felt bloated and terribly uncomfortable after one cup of milk in the morning because it produced so much gas in his stomach. He was so unlucky!) They dressed very simply, usually a pair of worn out blue jeans, shirts, and sports shoes. They changed shirts every day. Jack's room was in a muddle, clothes, books and exercising equipment spread all over the floor. Jim was much better in this respect, keeping his room tidy and clean, even with a few pots of flowers, so one would feel very comfortable and fresh whenever entering his room.

On weekdays the tenants seldom met each other. But on weekends Xiao K had to put up with a lot. There were frequent parties, usually five or six men and women gathered together in Jack's room, and sometimes in the garden. They had barbecues with salads and drank a lot of beer, sang and played rock music for all hours. It seemed that the ceiling of the house would be lifted apart. Jack was both talkative and active. He could play electric guitar very well. But Xiao K guessed that his studies were not as excellent as his guitar playing because Jack once carelessly mentioned that he got an "F" last semester, and had to do the same subject again. Jim was comparatively reticent, honest and simple. Jack always teased him with his nickname "Fatty," but he was never irritated. Jack said Jim was a good student with 3.5 average. The two got on well with each other. There was only one exception — when Jack's girlfriend came Jim never interrupted them but stayed in his own room. This probably is the thing called privacy.

Within about five days, Xiao K had a general knowledge of his housemates. Then he planned his strategy for associating with them. He would stay a "respectful" distance from Miss Z in case she pestered him and wasted his valuable time. One morning he was having his breakfast, Miss Z entered the kitchen in a hurry, blushing scarlet with excitement. She told him that she had had a divination — she could find a perfect husband by the end of this year. (If Heaven had eyes, Miss Z would have found the right person for she was incomparably pious. She had a statue of Buddha in her room and worshipped it every day, with incense smoke curling up. In this respect, she was not Westernized at all.) She was so talkative that Xiao K almost missed a lecture.

As for the two gentlemen, he decided to chat with them as much as possible on weekends in order to get more knowledge of American college students. Both of them were straightforward and always said what was really on their minds. They would not say "yes" if they did not agree with your opinion and they never hid their real thoughts. Another characteristic different from Chinese was that they did not like to inquire about others' privacy. Maybe that would be regarded as "cold" by Chinese. Well, that depends upon how you explain it. Chinese do really care about each other, and sometimes with extraordinary zeal so that the one who is cared for does not know how to react. The invisible pressure can make one restless, reluctant to go to work, apathetic or even mentally deranged. In Xiao K's opinion, Westerners' "coldness" is also worthy of being learned. Why does one have to disclose his private life to the public? Isn't it better to change this sort of Chinese custom in the future? Xiao K did not mean to criticize the socialist morality of caring for and helping each other, but it should have limits.

Studying in America would be totally different than at home. Xiao K could not predict how it would turn out, although he did know that the Chinese students who had come earlier were excellent, almost all got straight A's. He was a "worker, peasant and soldier" college student. He had entered university without taking any entrance examinations during the "cultural revolution," which means he had not learned as much as the normal students and could not compete with those from famous universities. There were so many elite students here — what was his position? But Xiao K knew clearly that he had no alternative but to go on. Otherwise he would not be able to face his family and friends for the rest of his life.

"Ideal is a torch and hope is power," Xiao K thus opened a new page as a student studying in the States.

图书在版编目(CIP)数据

中国人眼里的西方人:英文/王建光编.

北京:外文出版社,1990(1995 重印)

ISBN 7－119－01216－9

Ⅰ.中… Ⅱ.王… Ⅲ.西方国家－生活方式－通俗读物

Ⅳ.C913

中国版本图书馆 CIP 数据核字(95)第 13854 号

中国人眼里的西方人

王建光　编

*

ⓒ外文出版社

外文出版社出版

(中国北京百万庄大街 24 号)

邮政编码 100037

北京外文印刷厂印刷

中国国际图书贸易总公司发行

(中国北京车公庄西路 35 号)

北京邮政信箱第 399 号　邮政编码 100044

1990 年(36 开)第 1 版

2000 年第 1 版第 4 次印刷

(英)

ISBN 7－119－01216－9/G·26(外)

01680

17－E－2503P